HAPPY THE PEOPLE

When Love Becomes Justice

Marie D. Hoff, PhD

Foreword by Marcella M. Wilske

Liguori
LIGUORI, MISSOURI

Imprimi Potest:
Harry Grile, CSsR, Provincial
Denver Province, The Redemptorists

Published by Liguori Publications
Liguori, Missouri 63057

To order, call 800-325-9521
www.liguori.org

Library of Congress Cataloging-in-Publication Data

Hoff, Marie D.
    Happy the people : when love becomes justice / Marie D. Hoff, PhD.—
First Edition.
        pages cm
    Includes bibliographical references.
    1. Social justice—Religious aspects—Catholic Church. I. Title.
    BX1795.J87H64 2013
    261.8—dc23

                      2012048028
p ISBN 978-0-7648-2233-9
e ISBN 978-0-7648-2285-8

Liguori Publications, a nonprofit corporation, is an apostolate of The Redemptorists. To learn more about The Redemptorists, visit Redemptorists.com.

Printed in the United States of America
17 16 15 14 13 / 5 4 3 2 1

First Edition

Contents

Dedication

TO MY SISTERS AND MY BROTHER,
with love, honor, and remembrance:
Lee Ann Hoff and Lee R. Hoff
and
Bernadine M. Hoff (RIP November 4, 2011)
James L. "Jim" Hoff (RIP December 12, 2010)
Kenneth M. "Ken" Hoff (RIP December 22, 2008)

Acknowledgments

MY MOST SINCERE THANKS to Erin Cartaya and the entire staff at Liguori Publications. I am grateful for your skilled and patient assistance. I thank Patricia Clark, who directed religious education at Corpus Christi Catholic Parish, Bismarck, North Dakota, for twenty-eight years. She connected me to Liguori and has offered friendship and support along the way.

Carol McGee, pastoral associate at Sacred Heart Catholic Church in Boise, Idaho, the members of "Little Way" small faith community, also from Sacred Heart, and Ellen Piper of the *Boise Catholic Worker* offered helpful comments on an early draft of the manuscript. I greatly appreciate your time and effort and your social-justice witness.

Peg Wuelfing, PhD, director of Mission Centered Education, Boise, Idaho, is a wonderful friend and gifted colleague. I am forever grateful for your detailed reading and helpful suggestions about both content and style, in addition to personal support and encouragement. To Sister Meheret Tzeggai, beloved Comboni missioner friend in Uganda, I send endless gratitude for faithful prayers and good works.

I thank all my friends and family for giving me endless support. To the unknown millions who toil in the vineyards of the Lord, giving generously of yourselves in living the gospel of love, justice, and peacemaking, thank you for inspiration and motivation. You are truly the children of God.

The Holy Spirit brought courage and inspiration along the way.

Happy the people who acclaim such a king,
who walk, O Lord, in the light of your face,
who find their joy every day in your name,
who make your justice the source of their bliss.

PSALM 89
FROM *LITURGY OF THE HOURS*,
WEDNESDAY OF THE TWENTY-THIRD WEEK IN ORDINARY TIME

Foreword

WHAT DOES IT MEAN to live a happy and holy life—a righteous life? This is a question that has perplexed and challenged people of faith throughout the ages. The prophet Micah tells us that the righteous person—the person in right relationship with God and with all of God's creation—is one who "acts with justice, loves tenderly, and walks humbly with God." I do not believe that Micah's use of such powerful action verbs is accidental. Called to be a prophetic voice in a turbulent world, Micah deliberately uses this type of terminology to remind us that we are called to be people who put our faith into action each and every day in the unique circumstances of our lives. Social action, especially on behalf of the poor and powerless, must be at the heart of who we are as people of faith—as covenant people.

Many Catholics generously put their faith into action by feeding the hungry, clothing the naked, sheltering the homeless, and providing other Corporal Works of Mercy that enhance the life and dignity of those in need. They are very familiar with the Church's call to practice works of love and charity and embrace their calling enthusiastically. The call to practice biblical justice, however, is far less familiar. In their 1998 document Sharing the Message of Catholic Social Teaching, the United States Catholic Bishops acknowledge this fact when they write: "Far too many Catholics are not familiar with the basic content of Catholic Social Teaching. More fundamentally, many Catholics do not adequately understand that the social teaching of the Church is an essential part of Catholic faith. This poses a serious challenge for all Catholics, since it weakens our capacity to be a Church that is true to the demands of the Gospel."

For years, Marie Hoff and I talked about different ways to help others come to a better understanding of and appreciation for our Church's social-justice teachings. What would be enticing? What would be nonthreatening? What would enjoyable and fun? While I pursued this in the vineyards of parish and diocesan ministry, Marie put her academic background to work and produced *Happy the People: When Love Becomes Justice.*

Happy the People provides an introductory study guide for individuals, high school students, small faith communities, RCIA groups, and others who are eager to learn the basics of Catholic teaching about social justice. By linking Catholic prayer, worship, Scripture, and Church documents with justice principles and values, Marie shows how the social teachings of our Church are not some recent "fad" but are authentic teachings that have been—and continue to be—central to our Catholic faith. In an easy-to-read and enjoyable style, she shows how our social teachings are not meant to be seen as lofty, dry, theological ideals, but as practical "road maps" to help people of faith live a holy, happy, and righteous life amidst the complexities of everyday human existence and experience. Reflection questions are also provided to further stimulate personal discussion, sharing, and growth.

Rather than simply expounding on the various Catholic Social Teaching principles, *Happy the People* brings the Church's call to biblical justice alive by providing practical examples of how all of us can better integrate justice into our prayer life and be those people of action we are called to be—people who live God's call to justice in our families, in our places of work, in our parish communities, and in our civic and political life.

In *Happy the People,* Marie reminds us that both love and justice are ultimately about relationships—our relationship to God and with one another. Which brings me back to the prophet Micah. The holy and happy person, Micah reminds us, is one who lives in "right relationship" with God and with one another. This is what it means to be a covenant people. May your reading of *Happy the People* enliven your faith, enhance your understanding of justice principles, enrich your community, and lead you to new and exciting ways of being in covenant relationship with God, with those around you, and with all of God's creation.

MARCELLA M. WILSKE, CHANCELLOR/PASTORAL CENTER DIRECTOR,
ROMAN CATHOLIC DIOCESE OF BOISE

Introduction

WHEN I WAS JUST SIXTEEN, a favorite teacher (Sister Margaret Ellen Traxler, SSND) from my Catholic high school in western North Dakota sent me across the state to attend a workshop on Catholic social-justice teachings. It was a very long trip, and I don't remember anything about Fargo. What I do remember is the sense of excitement I experienced from the week-long "Chautauqua" with Father Louis Twomey, a well-known Jesuit from Loyola University of New Orleans. He was traveling around the country that summer introducing high school students to Catholic Social Teaching. I have carried my enthusiasm for the Church's teachings and my life's passion for justice ever since.

However, in those days, we were not so well taught what to do with the wonderful knowledge presented—how to get practical about taking action for justice. I thrashed around for years trying to find how to put these justice principles and values into action and integrate them with my basic Catholic faith commitments to prayer, charity, and service. This book was written with the goal of helping others gain an understanding of the Church's social teachings a whole lot faster than I did.

In this book I attempt to do three things: provide an introduction to the social teachings of the Church; relate these teachings to Scripture, prayer, and liturgical worship; and give some basic information on how to take action for justice, in conjunction with your own local parish, but also in your work and civic life.

As a beginning introduction to the social teachings of the Church, this brief volume can be read individually; the prayers and reflection questions in each chapter can help you deepen your understanding. It is also designed for a small faith community where you can pray together and gain enriched understanding through discussion and exchange of life experiences. It would also serve well for general parish faith formation groups, for young adults, or for people new to the Catholic tradition, such as RCIA candidates.

An important understanding I have gained of justice as a Christian virtue is that it is grounded in Scripture and integrally linked to the worship and prayer life of the Church. This book takes a distinctive approach in linking the study of the Church's social teachings to Scripture and worship. Each chapter includes discussion of scriptural foundations and suggestions for scriptural readings related to the topic under review. Each chapter begins with suggested songs/hymns and beautiful prayers used at Masses throughout the liturgical year that express the chapter's main theme in more poetic form. Of course, if used in a group it is quite all right to substitute or supplement with other relevant prayers or hymns.

Each chapter includes a brief introductory narrative, followed by a summary of a major social-teaching document that addresses the theme of the chapter. It is my hope that you will be motivated to seek out and read some of the original messages written by the popes and bishops over the past 125 years of modern Catholic social-justice teachings. The questions for reflection and discussion at the end of each chapter are intended to stimulate and guide your deeper exploration of the ideas presented; you may well come up with better questions of your own to pursue.

The reference list is supplemented with a few suggestions for additional readings on various facets of justice discussed in the book. The appendices include additional resources to help you with your study and action for justice, such as books, films, and contact information for Catholic organizations.

I sincerely hope my efforts in this book will save you the many years of struggle I had, that it will assist and enliven your commitment to incorporating justice into your Christian practice of prayer, family life, civic participation, and daily work.

CHAPTER ONE

Justice and Peace Will Kiss: Overview of Sources for Catholic Teachings on Justice

Suggested Opening Song: "Let Us Build the City of God" (*Gather Comprehensive Hymnal* #678) or "God Whose Purpose Is to Kindle" (*Gather Comprehensive Hymnal* #714)

Opening Prayer: Let us pray [that our prayer rise like incense in the presence of God]

Pause for silent prayer

Almighty Father,
strong is your justice and great is your mercy.
Protect us in the burdens and challenges of life.
Shield our minds from the distortion of pride
and enfold our desire with the beauty of truth.
Help us to become more aware of your loving design
so that we may more willingly give our lives in service to all.
We ask this through Christ our Lord.

The Sacramentary, Alternative Opening Prayer,
Thirty-Second Sunday in Ordinary Time

Gospel Reading: Luke 4:16–21 (Jesus announces his mission to bring freedom from oppression.)

Thematic Quote From Document:

"The joys and the hopes, the grief and anguish of the people of our time, especially of those who are poor or afflicted, are the joys and hopes, the grief and anguish of the followers of Christ as well.

Nothing that is genuinely human fails to find an echo in their hearts. For theirs is a community of people united in Christ and guided by the holy Spirit in their pilgrimage towards the Father's kingdom, bearers of a message of salvation for all of humanity. That is why they cherish a feeling of deep solidarity with the human race and its history."

PASTORAL CONSTITUTION ON THE CHURCH IN THE MODERN WORLD (*GAUDIUM ET SPES*), 1, VATICAN COUNCIL II

Background Narrative

Several years ago, while I was offering a workshop on Catholic social-justice teachings at a diocesan education event, a participant in the group spoke up to say, "That word—*justice*—makes me very uncomfortable. Can't you find another word?" How can a contemporary Catholic grow in understanding that being a disciple of Jesus means being a person of justice?

Various meanings of justice: Yes, justice is a loaded word, with many positive and negative connotations. To some it simply means the punishment and retribution due to people who have gravely violated the rights of others, as in, "I want justice." To others it may conjure unpleasant thoughts of the governmental system for keeping law and order in society, as in, "The United States Department of Justice." However, to the poor, to those who feel neglected or shut out by the rest of society, "justice" may arouse cynicism or anger, or even a sense of despair that they might ever have the means to enjoy the good things of society. So how can the psalmist in the Bible's *New Revised Standard Version* see justice as the source of our joy (Psalm 89:14–15) rather than as an uncomfortable word? Why does Jesus say those persecuted for justice will inherit the "kingdom of heaven" (Matthew 5:10)?

In Scripture and in our Catholic tradition, "justice" contains and points toward a vision of the entire foundation and universal range of our Christian faith. This is because, in Scripture, justice is seen as right relationships (Mott, 1982; Donahue, 2004). "Right relationship" means good and positive relationship with God, with our fellow human beings (most especially the poor and powerless), and with all of God's creation—marked by mutual respect, love, and concern. Peace is the result of such relationships, as the psalmist poetically envisions: "Love and truth will meet; justice and peace will kiss" (Psalm 85:11).

Justice has always been a central concern of the Church, even though the terminology and the particular issues have varied greatly over the centuries. For example, in the early centuries of the Church, before Christians had any control over public governmental institutions, they usually saw justice as the duty to reach out to the poor and needy directly with charity and generosity. But even in those early centuries, based on the teachings of Jesus and the Apostles, Church leaders taught that the noble vocation of Christians is to do our part to promote the rule of Christ on earth, where God "will wipe every tear from their eyes, and there shall be no more death or mourning, wailing or pain, [for] the old order has passed away" (Revelation 21:4). Saint Peter urges the new Christians "to be, conducting yourselves in holiness and devotion, waiting for and hastening the coming of the day of God, because of which the heavens will be dissolved in flames and the elements melted by fire. But according to his promise we await new heavens and a new earth in which righteousness dwells" (2 Peter 3:11–13).

The modern Church addresses justice: Most historians would agree the modern age for the Western world began with the American Revolution, followed quickly by the French Revolution. These political revolutions (which gradually gave people expanded voice in their own governments) were closely accompanied by the scientific and industrial revolutions (which gave humanity vastly greater power over the natural world). All these social changes have had profound impacts on the Catholic Church—its understanding of itself and its role in the world.

During the nineteenth and early twentieth centuries, the first issue Catholic leaders struggled to respond to was the Church's relationship and duties toward the newly emerging urban working classes, primarily in Europe, who were deeply oppressed in the horrifying working conditions in the factories and mines of the burgeoning modern industrial system. Wages were extremely low, long working hours and unsafe working conditions contributed to frequent injury and early death for men, women, and even very young children.

Economic theories and systems—such as socialism, Marxism/communism and capitalism—challenged the Church to address the fundamental social-justice principles at stake in each of these theories, and their role in the severe injustices found in actual social and economic activity (Cort, 1988). (These principles will be summarized in chapter two).

Contemporary teaching sources: Church response to the justice demands and religious meanings of these new social, economic, and political realities has resulted in a comprehensive and well-respected body of teachings put forth by popes and bishops over the past 125 years. These documents are typically referred to as modern Catholic Social Teachings. The first of the papal documents to address modern social and economic conditions was Leo XIII's *Rerum Novarum* (Of New Things, 1891).

Church leaders have gone on to address many other facets of modern economic and political life, such as racism, war and peace, poverty, private property, international debt, and development for poor nations, technology and the dignity of human work, migration and refugees, the fundamental importance of the Christian family, and respect for the earth's natural environment. A more recent papal commentary on social and economic concerns is Benedict XVI's *Caritas in Veritate* (Charity in Truth, 2009), which emphasizes how work for justice and human development must be rooted in Christian commitment to love and truth.

Typical teaching documents include (A) encyclicals, published by the popes (an open letter meant to be circulated to all Catholics and other people of good will); and, (B) pastoral letters, developed by individual bishops, or by national or regional conferences of bishops. Some exceptionally influential pastoral letters on social concerns of recent decades include the U.S. bishops' pastoral letters on nuclear war ("The Challenge of Peace," 1983) and on the American economy

("Economic Justice for All," 1986). Likewise, bishops in other parts of the world, such as Latin America and Asia, have offered pastoral teachings applying the gospel to social conditions in their own respective cultures.

Additional important sources for Catholic Social Teachings include the documents developed at Vatican Council II, which addressed the Church's relationship to the modern world, such as the Pastoral Constitution on the Church in the Modern World (1965), and Declaration on Religious Freedom (*Dignitatis Humanae*, 1965), as well as the pronouncements of universal or regional synods, such as the document titled *Justice in the World* from the world Synod of Bishops (1971). The *Compendium of the Social Doctrine of the Church* (Pontifical Council for Justice and Peace, 2004) is a comprehensive encyclopedia of the Church's social teachings, issued by the Vatican.

When the pope, an individual bishop, or a group of bishops develops a social encyclical or pastoral letter, they are assisted by theologians and others with academic knowledge and professional skills in, say, political and social science or economics. Collectively, they also draw on Scripture and the Church's deep 2,000-year tradition of knowledge and experience to explore how the gospel message may be lived out authentically in the actual conditions we experience in today's world. For example, Catholic bishops of seven Northwest dioceses, spanning the U.S. and Canada, developed a religious reflection on the moral and spiritual issues at stake in the future of the Columbia River and related water resources in the Northwest (Columbia River Watershed, 2001). Likewise, bishops in Appalachia have addressed social-justice concerns in their region, such as race relations and working conditions in meat processing plants.

Where we practice justice: Most basically, as disciples of Jesus, we must practice justice toward our own family, friends, and in our workplace. Church teaching also encourages Catholics to be active citizens participating, according to one's abilities, in civic life and other locally organized justice advocacy groups, for example, a local or national anti-poverty or anti-violence campaign. Chapter ten and the appendices in this volume discuss and offer additional resources and suggestions on how to build on prayer and study in order to begin to turn your social-justice beliefs into action—in your own life and in the larger world.

Charity vs. Justice? What are the differences and relationships between charitable work and work for social justice? Both are needed, and both express vital Christian values and virtues. A simple story is frequently used to help understand the difference:

> *Some folks are desperately pulling drowning victims out of a river and they become very weary. Finally, someone volunteers to go upstream and discovers a broken bridge. While many of those emergency workers necessarily continue pulling out the victims already in the river, at least some people get busy posting warning signs, collecting money for supplies and permanently fixing the bridge. The people pulling out the drowning victims can finally rest!*

Just so, in the Exodus story Moses tells Pharaoh, "Let my people go" (5:1). Moses demands their freedom, not better rations or fewer beatings for the slaves! Jesus too announces the beginning of his public ministry by quoting Isaiah's prophecy that he has come "to bring glad tidings to the poor"..."to proclaim liberty to captives" and "to let the oppressed go free" (see Luke 4:18–19). Jesus teaches, consoles, and heals, but he also rebukes the powerful for oppressing the poor, and he boldly proclaims God's kingdom—the reign of justice.

To use a traditional Christian image, charity is the crown of Christian virtue: it is direct giving of oneself to help others in need. Justice, however, is the foundation of charity: ensuring that society's laws, policies, and daily practices guarantee fairness and equity in how all members of society relate to one another. Thus, justice requires group and community organizing efforts to change specific laws and practices that result in indignities, human rights violations, and lack of life's necessities for vulnerable members of society.

Here are a few examples from recent and current history:

- During the era of racial segregation in America, no doubt many white people tried to treat black people with a measure of decency, and many practiced charitable acts such as helping a child obtain library books or giving food to a destitute family. But only major political changes, such as the Voting Rights Act and the outlawing of segregation, gave African Americans a real chance at basic justice. Legal changes also gradually helped change cultural attitudes so African American people no longer face daily insults or limitations that were not strictly "illegal," but which certainly did not respect their God-given human dignity.
- Similarly, activists in domestic violence organizations provide shelter and legal aid to battered spouses. They also advocate for stronger laws that protect women (and, in some cases, men) from domestic abuse and they work to change social attitudes that permit or encourage such illegal and immoral behavior.
- Catholics in the United States and other wealthier nations send much financial aid to people in poor nations, but it is equally important to work for just trade policies and resources to help poor nations build their own sustainable economic system.
- Charity cannot be perfect unless justice is also pursued.

Psalms and Reflections

Psalm 85:8–13 (A vision of the just society where love, justice and peace embrace.)

Wisdom 9:1–4, 9–10 (God's wisdom will help us as we seek understanding and work for just government.)

Baruch 5:1–4 (To live in peace is to be clothed in God's beauty and glory.)

Matthew 5:1–12 (Jesus teaches the way to true happiness or blessedness.)

The Documentary Heritage

—*Gaudium et Spes* (*GS*, Joy and Hope), Vatican Council II, 1965

Gaudium et Spes are the opening words of a major Vatican II document titled Pastoral Constitution on the Church in the Modern World. In this document the council Fathers put forth their teaching on how the Church and her spiritual mission relates to the contemporary world. David Hollenbach has declared it to be "the most authoritative and significant document on Catholic Social Teaching issued in the twentieth century" (2004, page 266).

Part 1 of *Gaudium et Spes* encourages Catholics to understand how life in this world relates to our striving for eternal life. It reviews the "signs of the times"—the economic, social, and political patterns of our contemporary world and notes the universal longing for greater opportunity and well-being (Introduction). Our efforts to improve social and economic conditions are not identical with, but they do contribute toward building the kingdom of God.

While noting the growing pluralism in beliefs and moral values in our contemporary world, (part 1, chapter 1) the council Fathers reiterate the enduring validity of human dignity and the need for humans to live and thrive in community (part 1, chapter 2). In part 1, chapter 3, *GS* states that human life in the world (the daily life of lay people) does have a religious significance because human creativity participates in God's creative action. Part 1, chapter 4 expresses a positive view of the relationship between the Church and other sectors of social life: the Church can learn from natural and social scientific knowledge; dialogue and interaction, not withdrawal from the world, is encouraged.

Part 2 of the document contains more specific discussion of Vatican II's teachings on modern social institutions and concerns, including marriage and family, cultural activity in society, economic life, modern political life, and the urgency of fostering peace and ending the arms race and international war. *GS* concludes by calling for Christians to participate in helping build up the international community to improve economic conditions and promote peace.

Additional Reading on the Role of the Church in the Modern World

—*Mater et Magistra* (Mother and Teacher), Pope John XXIII, 1961

Suggested Topics for Reflection and/or Discussion

1. What new understanding or insight did this chapter give you about the Christian meaning of *justice*? What similarities and differences did you see between secular or everyday use of the word and the meaning it carries in Scripture and Church teachings?
2. Identify one idea most interesting or important to you from the above discussion and from quotations or summaries of Church documents.
3. Reflect on an experience of injustice—(by yourself, a friend or neighbor, a family member (perhaps even a historical example from a grandparent's life). How does the religious meaning of justice as "right relationships" help you with your understanding of the kind of injustice you described? What kind of relationship was violated?
4. Read aloud how Jesus proclaimed his mission in Luke 4:16–21. In our present world, including your own local community, who do you see in need of liberation from poverty, oppression, blindness, etc.? As a Christian, how do you see yourself helping to minister to the "grief and anguish" of such oppressed groups or individuals?

Action Step

This week I will....(for instance, choose one idea to learn more about, or read and prayerfully reflect on a scriptural reading suggested by the chapter narrative).

Closing Prayer

Repeat the opening prayer, sing a song, or share an alternative prayer of your own choosing.

CHAPTER TWO

This We Believe: Social-Justice Foundations and Values

Suggested Opening Song: "You Are the Voice" (*Gather Comprehensive Hymnal* #549) or "We Are Called" (*Gather Comprehensive Hymnal* #718)

Opening Prayer: Let us pray [to our Father who has raised us to life in Christ]

Pause for silent prayer

Eternal Father,
reaching from end to end of the universe,
and ordering all things with your mighty arm:
for you, time is the unfolding of truth that already is,
the unveiling of beauty that is yet to be.
Your Son has saved us in history
by rising from the dead,
so that transcending time he might free us from death.
May his presence among us
lead to the vision of unlimited truth
and unfold the beauty of your love.
We ask this in the name of Jesus the Lord.

The Sacramentary, Alternative Opening Prayer, Seventh Sunday of Easter

Gospel Reading: John 8:31–32; John 16:12–13; John 18:37
(We can trust that Jesus teaches truth, and truth brings freedom.)

Thematic Quote From Document:

> *The foremost duty, therefore, of the rulers of the State should be to make sure that the laws and institutions, the general character and administration of the common wealth, shall be such as of themselves to realize public well-being and private prosperity....A State chiefly prospers and thrives through moral rule, well-regulated family life, respect for religion and justice, the moderation and fair imposing of public taxes, the progress of the arts and of trade, the abundant yield of the land —...And the more that is done for the benefit of the working classes by the general laws of the country, the less need will there be to seek for special means to relieve them.*
>
> RERUM NOVARUM, (ON CAPITAL AND LABOR),
> LEO XIII, 1891, SECTION 32

Background Narrative

During the extraordinary flooding along the Missouri River in 2011, a dramatic photo appeared on the front page of our local newspaper: An entire large home was pictured disappearing under the swirling powerful waters of the river. Many other homes and business buildings in several states were also totally destroyed during this major flood. In the parable of the man who built his house on sand (Luke 6:46–49), Jesus teaches us that we need to build our lives on firm foundations if we are to survive the mighty forces that challenge us: fearsome events of nature, as well as many momentous social and political changes and ethical questions in our contemporary world.

In this chapter I review a number of the key beliefs, values, and ethical principles that provide a firm foundation for Catholic Social Teachings. These core ideas help us understand why the Church takes a certain direction or position when teaching on more concrete or specific concerns that arise in today's world. For example, the principle of human dignity and the value of seeking the common good influence Catholic approaches to the current contentious policy issues of illegal immigration and how to ensure healthcare for all.

The human person is "trinitarian": The Church's social teachings are founded on a deep insight into how we as humans mirror the Trinity (distinctive persons within a community of perfect love and unity). This understanding balances the profound dignity—and inalienable human rights—of the individual with an equally important stress on our human need to live interdependently in community with other persons. Our human identity as an "Image of God" is properly formed and truly fulfilled only through constructive and happy relationships with other people. Happily, research from psychology, medicine, and many other sources confirms this assertion.

In contrast to the Catholic value of community, most Americans have a deeply ingrained philosophy of individualism that permeates our attitudes toward laws and policies and our daily behavior, whether we are aware of our underlying assumptions or not. When public policy proposals come up, such as laws to increase environmental protections or to increase taxation for schools, instinctively most of us first ask, "how will this affect me," rather than, "how will this serve to increase or decrease the common good of the whole community." Individualism also influences if we tend to blame others for personal failure or if we can also see how society contributed to their condition.

The Church sees the family as the first community (fundamental and necessary) in which we learn how to be human, that is how to live in harmony with other people. The basic theme, marbling its way through all of Catholic Social Teaching, is exactly this high-wire act of a vision of family, local, national, and world community in which the needs and rights of every human individual are balanced and respected within the peaceful and purposeful functioning of communities. As on the scales of justice, it doesn't work properly without the balance. Only in societies that respect individual rights, while simultaneously seeking the common good of all, can human beings become the kind of persons God means us to be. As Catholics, we believe we go to God together. (The balancing and interdependence between the individual and community is discussed in chapters four and five.)

The human family is one: Closely related to belief about the individual and the community is our Christian view of one universal human family. Pope John Paul II frequently used the term solidarity to express this belief. Through Jesus' final command to go and teach all nations and the experience of Pentecost, the early Church realized that God's redemptive work in Jesus is for all humanity. Just as any respectable, loving family takes special care of its weaker members—such as children or frail elderly—so the social teachings of the Church press us to have special concern for the vulnerable and poor. We are urged to see "the least among us" as brothers and sisters—and to pursue social and political policies that support the eradication of poverty throughout the world. (Poverty and international social solidarity among peoples are addressed in chapter seven.)

God is incarnate in creation: The Catholic Church is a "worldly" Church! By this I mean the Church insists that life in this world is important and even sacred, for the simple reasons that earth is where God has placed us to live, and God has joined us here in the Incarnation of Jesus. Some Christian sects (such as the ancient gnostics, and contemporary fundamentalist groups preoccupied with the "rapture") dismiss the importance of our human life on this earth, and the value of continuation of nonhuman life on the earth. I once saw a bumper sticker on a car that said, "Better to roast on earth than to fry in hell" (meaning that the phenomenon of climate change is of no concern—just avoid going to hell!). As Catholics we hope and trust we are destined for an unimaginably joyous future life with God, but meantime our life on this very material earth is also meaningful and important in its own right, because God made it and abides here with us through all of time.

All creation and human work participate in God's holiness: Two related principles flow from the belief that God dwells within creation: (A) All of creation has a universal and eternal destiny, according to Psalm 33:11: "But the plan of the LORD stands forever, the designs of his heart through all generations." (This belief will be explored in more depth in chapter eight on "Creation Care.") (B) Because life on earth is important and sacred, there is a distinction but no absolute separation between sacred and secular.

Here we have another example of the careful balancing that frequently occurs in Catholic Social Teaching: We respectfully maintain the proper distinctions between activities we deem to be "religious" and those that we deem to be "secular"—most especially our daily work. Nevertheless, we also believe secular activities have a sacred dimension when we direct our efforts toward benefiting other people and respecting the natural world. In our daily secular work we contribute toward bringing about the kingdom of God when we conduct ourselves with "integrity and justice" (Hosea 2:19). (The relationship between the sacred and secular is discussed in chapter five on the role of government in society to meet the common good, and in chapter six on the holiness of human work and the demands of economic justice.)

The sometimes angry rhetorical tone in American politics exemplifies how difficult it is to solve social problems, to respond to real needs in our society when we can't seem to find common ground in shared beliefs or values. The Church's social documents repeatedly call for commitment to dialogue and sincere listening to find our shared values across religious and other social divisions to meet common human needs (*Caritas in Veritate*, paragraphs 57–59).

We have access to Truth: The Catholic Church is profoundly countercultural in our belief that there is ultimate truth. (Many people nowadays believe all truth is relative or subjective—it's your personal choice.) While the Church's teachings are bedrock on principles, it is acknowledged that there is room for different opinions on how to apply them to solve concrete and complex problems in society. The Church acknowledges its primary leadership role in public policy debates is to educate and advocate for the basic principles of social justice. The informed conscience of lay Catholics and the legitimate knowledge of experts in a field of knowledge (such as medicine, law, economics, social welfare) must also be respected in efforts to meet social needs and redress social injustices. Clearly we don't have all the practical answers, and we are well-advised to maintain humility about our own grasp of social problems. Nevertheless Catholics—clergy and laity—have much to contribute to promoting justice in our society.

Justice and charity are related but distinct activities: The relationship between justice and charity is a complex theme permeating the social teachings of the Church. In the Bible (as discussed in chapters one and three), "justice" describes a situation where good and fair ("right" or "righteous") relationships exist between and among people. A just man—such as Saint Joseph—is one who practices fairness, respect, and concern toward all others. The Bible does not define justice in a dictionary kind of way, nor does it make keen distinctions between the practice of justice and the practice of charity. The two great commandments in both the Jewish and Christian Scriptures are to love God and neighbor. Such love is realized when we act in practical ways to give our neighbor what is his or her due: basic needs such as water and food, just wages, respect, freedom from abuse, and immediate help when he or she is in need. We might here remember Jesus' answer to the question of who is my neighbor in his story of the Good Samaritan on the road to Jericho (Luke 10:25–37).

In contrast, the Catholic philosophical tradition, traced back to Saint Thomas Aquinas, defines justice in more abstract categories. Social teachings use these categories to talk about these components of basic justice:

1. Distributive justice is fairness and equity in people's access to the necessities of life, including food, water, shelter, education, health-care, and work.
2. Commutative justice is fairness in exchange—contractual relationships (especially in work and economic exchanges) are balanced in the rights and responsibilities of each party—one side doesn't exploit the other party because of greater power or knowledge. Employers usually have more power than employees.

3. Participatory justice is fairness in people's ability to participate in decisions that affect them, especially in public life or in the workplace. Participatory justice means all people—not just those with the loudest voices or the most money—have a right to have some input and control over conditions of their own lives, especially in the workplace and civic (political) decision-making.

Like a diamond that sparkles when expertly cut, society flourishes when charity (love of neighbor) and these three facets of justice are realized for everyone: social justice, the common good, societal peace, are the ideal results when all persons experience these forms of justice (Hollenbach, 1977, pages 219–220). Following Saint Augustine, the Church frequently refers to this desired state of society as "the tranquility of order" (*City of God*, Book 19, chapter 13). (Dedicated work for building a peaceful society based on justice will be summarized in chapter nine.)

The linkages between charity and justice remain strong in current Catholic social ministries. Direct, loving service of neighbor will always be the keystone characteristic of true Christian life. But charity cannot achieve its crowning Christian meaning unless it is based on the foundation of justice—fairness, equity, and respect written into the laws and customs that guide our life in community. (The relationship between charity and justice in current Church teaching and ideas for individual and collective action will be discussed in more detail in chapter ten.)

Changes in perspective: Core Catholic beliefs and practices can be traced authentically to the gospel and through centuries of education, lived experience, and practice. However, some perspectives and emphases have changed or have been deepened as the Church has responded to changing social and economic realities in the contemporary world:

- After World War II the Church gained a greater awareness of being a truly global body—the traditional European perspective widened to include appreciation of other cultural ways of being. Social teaching expanded to address racism, Third-World poverty, and the imperative to reform international trade and financial systems to help poor nations succeed in social development.

- World War II also helped the Church move from a belief in monarchy as a God-given form of governance—and from foremost concern with maintaining traditional stability in society—to become a major advocate for democracy, freedom, justice, and universal human rights

- With the demise of communism, Catholic Social Teaching has placed more emphasis on the excesses of capitalism, stressing that private property rights are not absolute. Material goods must be used justly and thoughtfully to achieve the social good of the entire community. Excessive consumerism is deplored.

- The Church encourages dialogue and respectful engagement with the secular world to study "the signs of the times" and work to infuse gospel values and social-justice principles into how we choose to respond to challenging cultural, political, and economic conditions.

- Most recently, Church leaders (particularly John Paul II, Benedict XVI, and various national bishops' conferences) have begun to address more extensively the justice implications of respect and care for the natural world.

Psalms and Reflections

Psalm 146:1, 2, 6–8, 8c, 9, 9c (God has special concern for the poor and oppressed.)

Wisdom 7:22, 27, 30; 8:7 (God's Holy Spirit teaches us justice and other virtues.)

Romans 12:9–13 (Christians are called to overcome evil with goodness.)

John 1:1–6; 3:31–36 (Jesus came to bear witness to the truth.)

The Documentary Heritage

—*Rerum Novarum* (*RN*, On Capital and Labor), Leo XIII, 1891

This encyclical is generally acknowledged as the beginning of the modern social encyclical tradition. The Latin words *Rerum Novarum* (of new things) refer to the profound changes occurring in society in the nineteenth century due to the industrial revolution, the rise of capitalism, socialism, and the political struggles related to these developments. Driven out from traditional feudal agriculture, workers (including women and children) found themselves trapped in extremely exploitative working conditions in the mines, quarries, and factories of the emerging industrial system. Church leaders were worried about the attraction of socialism as an answer to the needs of the new urban workers. Nineteenth-century socialism advocated class warfare, an end to private property, and was typically critical of the Church for its perceived alliance with the rich and upper classes of society.

In *Rerum Novarum*, Leo XIII addresses a number of key points that have had enduring value and influence in the teaching of Catholic social justice, particularly with regard to economic and workplace justice. These include:

(A) Just wages are defined as an amount to enable a worker to support a family and live in frugal decency (paragraph 20). Just wages are an expression of both distributive and contractual justice, and they contribute toward the common good of the whole society (paragraph 27).

(B) Decent working conditions include reasonable hours of work, a day of rest, protection for women workers, along with a call to reduce child labor.

(C) Workers have a natural right to form associations (a precursor to the notion of trade unions). Leo notes that such workers' groups are legitimate and natural ways for them to assist each other to promote mutual well-being. Those who work so hard for the benefit of the entire community should themselves share in those benefits (paragraphs 48–51).

(D) The state has a legitimate role to regulate economic relationships to reduce poverty and protect workers. This is a new (and to some people startling) assertion by the pope that society doesn't just exist naturally, but is formed by the collective actions of people. In addition to Christian charity toward the poor, Leo XIII calls for government action to promote the general well-being of all members of society.

(E) There is a natural right for everyone to private property. In *Rerum Novarum*, Leo sees the need and rights of workers to have enough private property—economic resources—to provide a home and a modicum of personal comfort for oneself and one's family. However, the difference between such personal property and ownership of large-scale industrial operations (what the socialists called "the means of production") is not yet explicitly discussed.

At this early stage of development of Catholic social thought, the immense and ever-increasing concentration of wealth and power in the upper classes of society is simply not yet recognized. Later encyclicals deepen the moral and spiritual criticism of extreme social and economic disparities in the world.

Additional Reading

—*Centesimus Annus*, Pope John Paul II, 1991

Suggested Topics for Reflection and/or Group Discussion

1. Reflect on some specific examples of ways in which your life has been enriched by your own experience of community (think of family, church, work, your geographic community, groups or organizations to which you belong).

2. Consider this "thought experiment" on individual vs. community ways to meet needs: Many people in America drink bottled water, either for convenience or because they believe it may be safer than

tap water. Yet bottled water is significantly more expensive than tap water, and repeated scientific studies indicate it is no safer. Moreover, the billions of plastic bottles threaten the natural environment (our shared earthly community). Think of some ways in which your local city or state could find more communal ways to help everyone participate to meet these two goals for our shared human need for water (convenience and safety) and the protection of the earth.

3. What one core idea or value seemed most interesting or important to you from the above discussion on basic beliefs?
4. Were you surprised to read about changes in the Church's perspectives after World War II? Which of these heightened or changed points resonates most closely with your own social concerns?

Action Step

This week I will....(for instance, read one of the original documents referred to in this chapter, write a note of thanks to someone who has been an important part of my experience of community, or pay special attention to news stories depicting people acting in a spirit of selfishness or a spirit of community).

Closing Prayer

Repeat the opening prayer, sing a song, or share an alternative prayer of your own choosing.

CHAPTER THREE

Your Word Is a Lamp: Biblical and Church Sources for Social Justice

Opening Song: "Lord You Give the Great Commission" (*Gather Comprehensive Hymnal* #456) or "Canticle of the Turning" (*Gather Comprehensive Hymnal* #556)

Opening Prayer: Let us pray [for the wisdom that is greater than human words]

Pause for silent prayer

Father in heaven,
the loving plan of your wisdom took flesh in Jesus Christ,
and changed [human] history by his command of perfect love.
May our fulfillment of his command reflect your wisdom
and bring your salvation to the ends of the earth.
We ask this through Christ our Lord.

The Sacramentary, Alternative Opening Prayer,
Sixth Sunday in Ordinary Time

Gospel Reading: Mark 12:28–34 (The two great commandments: to love God and neighbor.)

Thematic Quote From Document:

Charity is at the heart of the Church's social doctrine. Every responsibility and every commitment spelled out by that doctrine is derived from charity which, according to the teaching of Jesus, is the synthesis of the entire law (see Matthew 22:36–40). It gives real substance to the personal relationship with God and with neighbor; it is the principle not only of micro-relationships (with friends, with family members, or within small groups) but also of macro-relationships (social, economic, and political ones). For the Church, instructed by the Gospel, charity is everything because as Saint John teaches (see John 4:8, 16)....everything has its origin in God's love, everything is shaped by it, everything is directed towards it. Love is God's greatest gift to humanity, it is [God's] promise and our hope.

CARITAS IN VERITATE (CHARITY IN TRUTH),
BENEDICT XVI, 2009, PARAGRAPH 2

Background Narrative

Biblical sources: Modern Catholic social-justice teachings are rooted in the grand themes of salvation history in the Bible, from Genesis to the Book of Revelation. The Bible is a story about relationships: stories of people down the centuries of time struggling to understand and appreciate God's relationship to the created universe, God's relationship to us as human beings, and vice-versa, how people are to live justly —that is, in "right relationship" to God and to the whole of creation.

The stories and events, the poetry and prayers of Scripture flow together to teach us to live in harmony with one another and with the earth. From this harmonious living we begin to experience the deep peace that we know as a loving relationship with the holy mystery we name as God. The biblical term "righteousness" is best understood as our notion of "justice" namely living in good, fair, and honest relationships with others.

Proof-texting: Sacred Scriptures are sometimes used as a weapon in battles over religion. Selected texts are waved about to prove a point of view on contemporary hotly contested issues, such as homosexuality, or as a justification for violence and warfare. This use of the Bible is called "proof-texting"—pulling out one or more isolated passages to prove a point of argument, distorting or even falsifying the broader and deeper meaning of Scripture. For example, in Boise, Idaho, a group of people has stood every Wednesday for more than ten years in witness against the death penalty. Recently a passerby yelled out, "Don't you know the Bible says, 'an eye for an eye?'" One of the witnesses responded, "Actually, that was said several hundred years before Jesus came. He said to love and forgive our enemies."

Scripture teaches how we are to live: Contemporary biblical scholarship has helped us better understand how the writings of Scripture are embedded in the historical cultural context in which they were written. For example, Deuteronomy commands killing both men and women found in adultery; Saint Paul exhorts slaves to obey their masters. (Jesus forgave the woman taken in adultery, and much later, in the nineteenth-century Christian abolitionists found Scripture to be their best argument against slavery.) While the whole of Scripture is inspired by God, writers from the seventh century BC or the first century AD were not given human knowledge beyond their own era, such as scientific discoveries about the physical age of earth or our contemporary understanding of God-given human rights: these grew gradually over many millennia of human efforts to understand God's will for how we are to treat one another.

Scripture makes frequent use of stories to illustrate a lesson. The important goal of scriptural study and prayer is to search for the underlying message about who God is and for how we ought to live—that is where the "truth" of the story lies. For example, the amusing story of Jonah, the reluctant prophet, clearly illustrates how all people struggle with serious moral and spiritual demands—sometimes we actively resist and "run away" from the voice of God in our lives. The story of Job is intensely compelling. It helps us grapple with the profound questions of why evil and suffering occur; the story helps many to better understand how to become aware of God's compassion in such experiences.

Scripture teaches that creation has a sacred meaning and purpose, to move us both individually and collectively toward a loving reunion with God, from whom comes all that exists. As a community of faith we have a great treasure from which we gain a sense of our own dignity and freedom as human beings. We draw hope, courage, and a direction for our lives. This message contrasts with many voices essentially telling us that the universe and human life is either absurd or meaningless, or perhaps even predetermined—thus lacking hope, dignity, and freedom.

Scripture shows God is active in human history: As Catholics we believe the deepest truth in the biblical story is that God brought forth, and continues to bring forth, all of creation with infinite love and goodness. The Bible does include many historical persons and events, but it also uses poetry, stories, letters, prophetic rhetoric, metaphors, aphorisms (for example, Proverbs), and other writing styles, all intended to help us achieve a deeper understanding of who God is and what it means to live justly—to be in right relationship to both God and all of creation.

The grand themes of Scripture are **creation, Exodus/Covenant,** and **prophecy** in the Jewish Old Testament; and **Incarnation, the teachings and life of Jesus, redemption/resurrection,** and **God's kingdom/end times** in the Christian New Testament.

Infused in all the varied writings of Scripture is the story of how God is deeply involved in the history of humanity, including the history of the earth and the cosmos: "For in him all the fullness was pleased to dwell, and through him to reconcile all things for him, making peace by the blood of his cross (through him), whether those on earth or those in heaven" (Colossians 1:19–20).

In Scripture, the themes of relationships (with God, with fellow humans, and with the earth and universe) are played to the tune of justice and charity as the great virtues that ensure those relationships are the just relationships desired by God. The biblical stories of creation teach us the inalienable dignity and sacredness of human beings. All creation shares this dignity and sacredness: God sees that all that was made is "very good" (Genesis 1:31). The doctrine of Incarnation teaches us that in the earthly, human person of Jesus, God has resanctified and reaffirmed the dignity of all creation, most especially human beings. These are the foundational principles in Catholic Social Teachings, calling us to social justice and to respect for creation.

Every year at the liturgies of Holy Week and Easter the Church reenacts the story of Jesus' suffering, death, and resurrection. Christ's sacred action continues to save and free us from the futility of death and brings us joy in the hope of genuine life both now and for eternity. During the Easter Vigil we also reread the stories of how God led the Hebrew people from slavery and oppression in Egypt (the Exodus), and how God taught the people through the forging of the covenant in the desert. The Israelites were taught the two great commandments. Having been delivered from slavery, they must now cultivate just relationships with one another through the command to love one's neighbor as oneself. This neighborly relationship is founded on mutual acknowledgment of God's preeminence in their lives: "Therefore, you shall love the LORD, your God, with your whole heart, and with your whole being, and with your whole strength" (Deuteronomy 6:5).

We all sin and fail to live up to right relationships of justice and love with God, neighbor, and creation. Through the teachings of the **prophets** and through the **life and teachings of Jesus** we learn of God's loving, patient efforts to call us back, like a loving spouse: "I will betroth you to me with justice and with judgment, with loyalty and with compassion" (Hosea 2:21). Gradually, the prophets bring us to a higher and purer understanding of "what the LORD requires of you: Only to do justice and to love goodness, and to walk humbly with your God" (Micah 6:8).

The denunciation of injustice and the summons to *do justice* permeate the lives and teachings of the prophets. Today such persons are called "social critics": Prophets point out a clarion-clear message: the disorder, the violence, the hatred, and other myriad evils in society result from people's failure to practice justice toward neighbors—especially from exploiting workers (cheating or failing to pay wages) and ignoring the poor and vulnerable among us. In Old Testament times these were usually the widows, orphans, and strangers; now we may also include other groups, such as people who are mentally ill, homeless, disabled, unemployed, or refugees and immigrants.

Jesus is indeed our greatest prophet, our best social critic, showing us how to move from injustice to justice. We learn from the model of his very life, as well as from his gospel teachings: Justice between neighbors is the very heart of true worship and godliness. Jesus takes the teachings about love of God and love of neighbor to new idealistic heights in which justice is crowned by divine charity. Saint Paul tells us, as Christians we are called to kenosis—the self-emptying **love** exemplified in the teachings, life, and death of Christ. By our own self-giving practice of compassion, love, and justice toward neighbor we die to sin and selfishness and participate in the deep peace and joy of imitating Christ (Colossians 3:12–17).

The coming of God's **kingdom** is proclaimed by Jesus in all the gospels. At Pentecost (called the birthday of the Church), the fearful, cowering disciples received the Holy Spirit of Jesus and were infused with the wisdom and courage of the Spirit to begin the Church's work of bringing about God's reign of peace and justice. In the Catholic interpretation of the end times we as followers of Christ receive the great commission to "go into the whole world and proclaim the gospel to every creature" (Mark 16:15).

In this way the grand themes of Scripture provide the foundation for modern Catholic Social Teachings and they give us the vision and inspiration to work toward building the world of love, the world of justice and peace that God desires. Sacred Scripture lays out the indispensible blueprint of our lived faith (Donahue, 1977; 2004).

Other foundations for Catholic Social Teachings: To strengthen our understanding of social justice we also use Church teachings based on our collective understanding gained over centuries of lived Christianity. We call this accumulated wisdom of the Church "tradition." So for example, as noted above, slavery was considered natural in the ancient world. Theological knowledge and human understanding gained through the ages have helped us understand how such a social practice is deeply at odds with the basic Christian belief that God desires mutual respect and justice between people.

We the Church, the community of the followers of Christ, must also use our God-given intelligence and life experience to understand how to live as followers of Christ in the changing circumstances of human history. The social teachings urge us to actively form our conscience for living a life of justice. The lives of saints and other Christian leaders also help us by giving us models of how to practice Christian discipleship; learning from their examples can be a great motivator. See Appendix C for names and resources to learn more about some contemporary social-justice saints and leaders.

In our times we are also fortunate to have access to the vast knowledge base of the natural sciences and social sciences, as well as humanistic studies (philosophy, history, politics, literature, etc.) to help us better understand how to bring about the kingdom of God envisioned in Scripture.

In summary of chapters two and three, Catholic Social Teaching draws on Scripture, Church tradition, accumulated human knowledge, and spiritual wisdom gained from people's actual lived experience to provide basic beliefs and values for our response to serious needs, problems, profound sufferings, and outright evils afflicting people today. Catholic social-justice teaching is widely regarded as the most comprehensive and coherent body of Christian teachings on this subject. It is a proud heritage given the Church to teach and put into practice.

Psalms and Reflections

Psalm 111:1–4, 7–10 (We ponder God's goodness and truth and offer heartfelt thanks.)

Luke 10:25–37 (Who is our neighbor? Anyone in need.)

Philippians 2:1–11 (We should imitate Christ's humility in our concern for others.)

Romans 11:33–36 (We can never fully understand the depths of God's wisdom.)

The Documentary Heritage

—*Caritas in Veritate* (Charity in Truth), Benedict XVI, 2009

In this brief, almost prayerful reflection, Pope Benedict utilizes basic Christian beliefs and values to illuminate some basic concerns in our contemporary world. He reviews trends in global social, political, economic, and technological realms. Then he beautifully explains how Christian understanding of charity and truth provide the framework for action that promotes integral human development (the whole person, including the spiritual and relational) and the common good of the human family. Without charity and truth, "social action ends up serving private interests and the logic of power" (paragraph 5). Truth, in his explanation of action in the social arena, is an orientation toward justice and the common good. In the social arena, charity or love is enacted when we form just social, economic, and political institutions.

Benedict wrote *Caritas in Veritate* to commemorate the publication of Pope Paul VI's great encyclical on international development, *Populorum Progressio* (1967). He strongly reiterates Paul's teaching that work for justice, peace, and the development of peoples (especially the poor) is an expression of Christian charity and the spread of the gospel (paragraph 15). He reminds governments that the "primary capital to be safeguarded is...the human person" (paragraph 25). Great progress has been achieved in meeting the legitimate needs and hopes of human communities in recent decades. The increasingly interconnected global communication, financial, and economic arenas have brought tangible benefits. Nevertheless, some current beliefs and unjust practices in the global scene present threats to human dignity, they lack attention to the whole person, and they may not even serve the best economic interests of nations or groups that promote them.

Some of the key concerns identified include:

(A) Damage to national social security systems and increasing powerlessness of workers when companies seek the lowest cost competitive production sites. Oftentimes, the cultural integrity of local communities is also threatened by global market competition.

(B) World hunger (food insecurity) remains a huge problem. All people have a basic right to food and water (paragraph 27). Poverty itself is a threat to life. Violence in the name of religion threatens life and religious freedom (paragraphs 28–29).

In today's world, justice requires both a decrease in wealth inequalities and "steady employment for everyone" (paragraph 32).

World development today must also address respect for the natural environment, a sober assessment of technological solutions, and a serious quest for new energy sources (paragraphs 48–51 and 68–77).

Government action is necessary to ensure a just and effective operation of the market economy. In addition, *Caritas in Veritate* articulates a key theme in the Catholic social tradition, namely the importance of civil society (nonmarket, nonstate) organizations and groups. Here, human solidarity and mutuality can grow and people can experience giftedness or gratuity—the richness of human experience beyond sheer competitive exchange. This sense of gratuity could also be increased in market settings by more attention to stakeholders, not just financial shareholders. New forms of development efforts, which mix profit with other not-for-profit goals, also present hope for increased gratuity.

Benedict concludes: "Openness to God makes us open towards our brothers and sisters and towards an understanding of life as a joyful task to be accomplished in a spirit of solidarity" (paragraph 78).

Suggested Topics for Reflection and/or Discussion

1. Reread a favorite story or teaching from Scripture, or one suggested above; describe how it helps you understand how to love your neighbor.
2. In the story of the Good Samaritan (Luke 10:25–37), Jesus teaches that everyone in need is our neighbor. How do you think this applies to our relationship to people in other countries, especially the poor nations of the world?
3. Read aloud and then spend some time reflecting on one brief passage that is most meaningful to you from this chapter's discussion on the scriptural and Church sources for understanding justice. (Read either the chapter narrative or the Church documents).
4. Describe one thing you strive to do in your daily life to actively contribute to bringing about the kingdom (rule) of God's love and justice. (This might be a practice you regularly observe in relationship to your family, your job, or perhaps a volunteer work commitment.)

Action Step

This week I will....(for instance, reflect and pray more deeply on a suggested passage regarding justice, look up more information on the Internet about world poverty or trade, or read this chapter a second time for new insights).

Closing Prayer

Repeat the opening prayer, sing a song, or pray an alternative prayer of your own choosing.

CHAPTER FOUR

Made in the Image of God: Human Dignity, Rights, and Responsibilities

Suggested Opening Song: "Whatsoever You Do," (*Gather Comprehensive Hymnal* #670) or "Where Charity and Love Prevail" (*Gather Comprehensive Hymnal* #625)

Opening Prayer: Let us pray [for the peace which is born of faith and hope]

Pause for silent prayer

Father in heaven, Creator of all,
look down upon your people in their moments of need,
for you alone are the source of our peace.
Bring us to the dignity which distinguishes the poor in spirit
and show us how great is the call to serve,
that we may share in the peace of Christ
who offered his life in the service of all.
We ask this through Christ our Lord.

The Sacramentary, Alternative Opening Prayer,
Twenty-Fourth Sunday in Ordinary Time

Gospel Reading: Matthew 5:1–11; 43–48 (Jesus teaches us how to treat other people.)

Thematic Quote From Document:

An act of the highest importance performed by the United Nations Organization was the Universal Declaration of Human Rights, approved in the General Assembly on December 10, 1948...the recognition and respect of those rights and respective liberties is proclaimed as a goal to be achieved by all people and all countries. ....The document represents an important step on the path towards the juridical-political organization of all the peoples of the world. For in it, in most solemn form, the dignity of a human person is acknowledged to all human beings; and as a consequence there is proclaimed, as a fundamental right, the right of every man freely to investigate the truth and to follow the norms of moral good and justice, and also the right to a life worthy of man's dignity, while other rights connected with those mentioned are likewise proclaimed...all human beings...are becoming more consciously aware that they are living members of the whole human family.

PACEM IN TERRIS, (PEACE ON EARTH),
JOHN XXIII, 1963, PARAGRAPHS 143–145

Background Narrative

Have you observed small children shriek with anger and indignation when they feel forced into something they don't want (such as food or bedtime)? As adults we too can remember experiencing similar feelings of anger and a sense of insult—perhaps even an urge to scream or strike out—when we feel our rights, freedom, or dignity have been violated. The bedrock foundation of Catholic Social Justice Teachings is belief in the innate dignity and sacredness of the human person. Our dignity is God-given, neither earned by our behavior nor bestowed by a benevolent government, or the respectful treatment of others. An unborn baby, a handicapped child, an elderly nursing home resident, a prisoner, an illegal immigrant, or a starving refugee each retain their innate dignity that we must honor, regardless of their status, behavior, or limitations.

Scriptural sources for human dignity: The story of creation stresses that we are made in the image of God. The story of Jesus tells us God became human (the Incarnation) to show us our own sacredness in our very bodily selves. Saint Paul stresses—with great vehemence—that we are the body of Christ. "There is neither Jew nor Greek, there is neither slave nor free person, there is not male and female; for you are all one in Christ Jesus" (Galatians 3:28). Therefore, we are called to extend to each other, and to every human being the same reverence and respect we feel toward Christ himself. The hymn "How Beautiful is the Body of Christ," based on Saint Paul's teaching, refers to Christ himself, as well as the beauty of all our human sisters and brothers. It takes daily practice to remember to always see the image of God, to respect the other person's dignity in our human encounters, most especially when we feel fear, repulsion, or anger toward him or her. Human dignity requires more than sheer avoidance of death or violence such as torture, slavery, human trafficking for labor or sex slavery, euthanasia, murder, spousal or child abuse, abortion, and other unspeakable violations of the human body, mind, and spirit. As Saint Irenaeus said in the second century AD, God wants us to flourish, to be fully alive.

Respect for human rights: Both Catholic teaching, such as the important encyclical *Pacem in Terris* (Peace on earth, 1963) and other sources, particularly the United Nations Universal Declaration of Human Rights (1948) spell out concretely some of the requirements for human dignity based on respect for our human rights: All people have a positive right to the resources needed to grow and to flourish as a fully developed person; people have a claim on enough food, clothing, education, housing, and healthcare to live decently. Employment (the right to work) enables people to develop their skills and abilities and to make a positive contribution to their community. Workers have a right to just wages, reasonable hours, and conditions of employment.

The Second Vatican Council passed a remarkable document titled *Dignitatis Humanae* (Human Dignity: Declaration on Religious Freedom, 1965). The statement based the Church's embrace of religious liberty on the principle of human dignity, which requires freedom from coercion in making choices. People have the freedom to practice their religion and to pass on their culture and religion to their children. Benedict XVI reiterates threats to religious liberty in our current context, namely using religion as a motive for violence, or making deliberate attempts to promote religious indifference or practical atheism (*Caritas in Veritate*, section 29).

People have a right to freely and safely participate in political activity. Catholic Social Teaching consistently states that human dignity requires that we have a meaningful role in the public policy decisions that affect our own lives. Governments have a duty to ensure that political corruption and manipulation do not enable the rich and powerful to control the public decision-making processes in their nations.

The Church's social teachings have stressed that human dignity means people have participatory rights to form workplace unions—to associate with other people to protect their own economic interests and decent workplace conditions. Reciprocally, unions have a duty to assess their demands in the light of the financial condition of their employer and of overall economic circumstances in the broader community, always looking toward the common good. Beyond their economic benefits, unions help serve a spiritual purpose by enabling people to form communities of concern for one another (solidarity) and mutual aid (Higgins, 1993).

People have rights to a basic sufficiency of private property that enables one to live in a dignified (though not luxurious) manner. However, private property rights are not absolute. The overall needs of the community—and the integrity of the natural world—must be taken into account when considering how to use one's private property. Dialogue and due process of law are essential for balancing competing values of property rights versus the legitimate needs and concerns of the community and society—the common good. For example, dangerous chemicals used in homes, farms, and factories have health impacts around the world when they eventually enter the air and water systems. Society has the duty and right—through scientific and political processes—to regulate the use of these dangerous substances.

The Church asserts people have basic rights of movement. We are neither slaves nor bound to the land like feudal serfs. In both Europe and North America where immigration is currently a burning political issue, Church leaders have recently spoken out urging governments to protect the human dignity of migrant workers and political refugees fleeing violence and possible death (see usccb.org/migration).

Beginning with Pope Leo XIII's 1891 encyclical *Rerum Novarum* (On Capital and Labor), social-justice teachings for many decades focused largely on the needs and rights of workers and on overall conditions in industrial workplaces. The rights of workers for just wages, reasonable work hours, and the ability to form unions were the Church's predominant human rights themes in the early stages of industrialization (nineteenth and early twentieth centuries).

New emphases after World War II: In the wake of World War II—with the revelation of the enormous scale of atrocities against human dignity and fundamental rights by the Nazi and Stalinist regimes—the Church began to emphasize a fuller range of human rights that must be respected to support the full flourishing of every human being. In 1962–63, world peace was threatened by the nuclear standoff between the United States and the Soviet Union. In this tense situation, Pope John XXIII issued a revolutionary encyclical titled *Pacem in Terris* (Peace on Earth, 1963). John XXIII believed world peace could not be realized without a worldwide commitment to human dignity and urgent action to protect the human rights of all people across the full spectrum of human activity—economic, social, religious, family, and political life (Christiansen, 2004).

Pope Paul VI continued to make the association between peace and human rights in the encyclical *Populorum Progressio* (Progress of People, 1967). His oft-quoted aphorism, "If you want peace, work for justice" (paragraph 76) summarizes the connection between peace and the means to achieve it—through promotion of the rights and the needs of all people, with special attention to the poor and disadvantaged.

Rights balance with responsibilities: Like a teeter-totter, it's a delicate balance to maintain. Because we believe in community, the Church takes a distinctive approach to human rights by stressing the balance with responsibilities. Odd as it may first sound, we have a duty to re-spect and exercise our own rights in a positive way. Reciprocally, we have a duty to defend and foster the full attainment of human rights by other people. Embracing these responsibilities we fulfill Saint Paul's admonition, "Bear one another's burdens, and so you will fulfill the law of Christ" (Galatians 6:2).

Our right to bodily respect and integrity means we have a justice duty to treat our own bodies with dignity, avoiding sins such as drugs, drunkenness, gluttony, promiscuity, reckless driving, and numerous other ways in which we violate our own dignity. We should assert ourselves in a nonviolent manner if others violate our dignity through abusive or exploitative behavior. We are bound to help ensure other people's bodily rights are respected. Examples might include protesting against torture or capital punishment, joining a group working to reduce child abuse and spousal violence, joining others to work for ensuring food, clean water, healthcare, and jobs for poor people.

Our right to participate in political decision-making is accompanied by our duty to vote and practice other forms of civic engagement within our personal capabilities and skills (such as becoming informed about issues, going to meetings, writing to elected officials, running for a public office, etc.). We have a duty to support and promote the participation rights of others, especially those most disadvantaged or powerless. A few examples might include supporting a local union organizing effort by service workers, speaking out and getting involved with groups that protect the rights of disadvantaged groups to vote, joining an international human rights group that monitors political rights under oppressive governments in other parts of the world.

Our economic rights to work and fair wages or profits are balanced by our duty to work to the best of our ability, to produce goods or services of genuine value for others, and to use our personal gifts to make a positive contribution to society. The Church considers work to include paid employment, self-employed economic endeavor, volunteer contributions, and family work such as raising children or caring for a disabled relative. Our duties to others also include supporting laws that set fair wages and taxes, as well as educational and training opportunities that enable everyone to contribute to society through useful work.

Examples of public support for human rights: Supporting others' rights may require being supportive of taxation for improved school systems or special job programs for adults struggling to find productive work in difficult economic times. Abolition of the death penalty in many states is partly attributable to public-advocacy efforts.

The work of Eunice and Sargent Shriver for persons with developmental disabilities is a marvelous example of advocacy for justice and human rights of a vulnerable group. As a result of their efforts, thousands of persons with developmental challenges work in sheltered workshops and other regular work settings; they experience pride in being able to contribute to society and to be like other people (Stossel, 2004). My own sister benefitted greatly from the Shrivers' persistent advocacy for programs to enable people with developmental disabilities to work and live like other people.

So, respecting human dignity requires more than merely being able to say at the end of the day, "Well, I didn't get drunk, steal, or yell at anyone today, or cut off another driver in a rude way, so I must be a pretty decent person." We must exercise our own rights and responsibilities in proactive ways and join with others in social-justice advocacy to ensure that human beings everywhere have their human rights and needs met so that all people can become the fully developed person in body, mind, and soul God meant them to be.

Of course, no one person can work on all issues of concern, but everyone can join some effort for human rights, whether through our parish or a larger community enterprise. In this way we are going to God together—promoting the peaceable kingdom of Christ where every person's sacred dignity is honored as "the one who sat on the throne said, 'Behold, I make all things new'" (Revelation 21:5).

Psalms and Reflections

Psalm 8:1, 3–5, 9 (A prayerful reflection offering praise to God for the immense dignity of being a human being.)

Genesis 1:26–27 (Male and female—we are created in God's own image.)

Genesis 4:9–12 (God says we are responsible for how we treat our fellow human beings.)

1 John 4:7, 12, 19–21 (We show our love for God by the love we show to others.)

The Documentary Heritage

—*Pacem in Terris* (*PT*, Peace on Earth), John XXIII, 1963

Just as *Rerum Novarum* stimulated Catholic participation in the labor movement, so *Pacem in Terris* is credited for Catholic action on human rights (Christiansen, 2004, page 217). The encyclical was published shortly before Pope John's death, at the height of the Cold War face-off between the USSR and the United States, amid a palpable fear that a nuclear holocaust could happen. His key message was that peace on earth can only be realized when the human rights of all persons are recognized and protected.

Human rights are based on our creation by God with intelligence and free will and on our universal redemption by Christ. *PT* discusses an extensive list of human rights: Some of these include the right to life and education, political rights (such as religious freedom and the right to assemble and participate in public life), economic rights (such as work and private property), and others. In contrast to the rather exclusive emphasis on rights in American public dialogue, *PT* expresses the Catholic balance and integration of rights with duties and responsibilities toward achieving the common good (Christiansen, page 226). In the positive tone reflecting his optimistic view of human nature, John reminds us that we are called to respect and foster the rights and freedoms of other people. A good society must indeed "function according to the norms of justice"...[and] be inspired and perfected by mutual love" (paragraph 37).

Aware of the "signs of the times" (that is, social trends), John XXIII affirms the particular human rights movements predominant in the 1960s: working class efforts for a better life, the struggles to end colonialism, women's assertion of equality, and the demand to end racial discrimination.

Toward the goal of world peace, *PT* recognizes the need for civil authority—government—to support human rights. Governance is legitimate only when people acknowledge its moral authority—"threats and fear of punishment...cannot effectively move men to promote the common good of all" (paragraph 48).

Pope John calls for strengthening international institutions, such as the United Nations, to address concerns beyond national states, such as political refugees and the arms race. (Author's note: Today we might include infectious diseases and environmental problems.) *PT* says international cooperation is also needed to ensure the rights of ethnic or other minorities within sovereign states, and to promote equity in trade and finance among powerful and less powerful nations. International public authority does not mean "one world government": The Catholic principle of subsidiarity means international authority should only tackle concerns that individual nations cannot solve on their own (paragraphs 140–141).

Additional Reading

—*Pontifical Council for Justice and Peace* (2004), "Creatures in the Image of God," *Compendium of the Social Doctrine of the Church*, pages 50–51

Suggested Topics for Reflection and/or Discussion

1. How do you see the relationship between rights and duties in your own life? What difference do you think it would make in American society if people more fully appreciated the relationship between rights and responsibilities?

2. In the United States, or in your own state or local community, which human rights do you see violated or disrespected? Identify the individuals or groups affected by these violations. What is being done or what do you think should be done to better ensure protection of these persons' human rights?

3. What can you do locally (as individuals or a parish or community group) in promoting human rights internationally? (See Appendix B for ideas and names of organizations.)

4. Reread aloud one brief passage from either the discussion or the papal documents above, and briefly describe what importance it has for you.

Action Step

This week I will....(for instance, try to identify human dignity or human rights violations that I observe in action or learn about from the daily news; join or send a donation to an organization working to protect human rights, such as a local domestic abuse shelter or an international human rights organization).

Closing Prayer

Repeat the opening prayer, sing a song, or share an alternative prayer of your own choosing.

CHAPTER FIVE

People Who Need People Are the Happiest People in the World: Community, Participation, and the Common Good

Suggested Opening Song: "We Are Many Parts" (*Gather Comprehensive Hymnal* #733) or "We Come to Your Feast" (*Gather Comprehensive Hymnal* #850)

Opening Prayer: Let us pray [to the Lord who is a God of love to all peoples]

Pause for silent prayer

Father in heaven,
the perfection of justice is found in your love
and all [human]kind is in need of your law.
Help us to find this love in each other
that justice may be attained
through obedience to your law.
We ask this through Christ our Lord.

The Sacramentary, Alternative Opening Prayer,
Twenty-Fifth Sunday in Ordinary Time

Gospel Reading: John 15:1–17 (Jesus is the true vine; in him we experience community and bear the fruit of love with one another.)

Thematic Quote From Document:

> ...*Democracies themselves...seem at times to have lost the ability to make decisions aimed at the common good. Certain demands which arise within society are sometimes not examined in accordance with criteria of justice and morality, but rather on the basis of the electoral*

or financial power of the groups promoting them. With time, such distortions of political conduct create distrust and apathy, with a subsequent decline in the political participation and civic spirit of the general population, which feels abused and disillusioned. As a result, there is a growing inability to situate particular interests within the framework of a coherent vision of the common good....

CENTESIMUS ANNUS (ON THE HUNDREDTH ANNIVERSARY), JOHN PAUL II, 1991, SECTIONS 47, 48

Background Narrative

In the classic book *Robinson Crusoe,* Daniel Defoe (1719) creatively explored how a castaway sailor survives on a deserted island. The highlight of the story is Crusoe's overwhelming joy when he discovers another human being on the island. The man he names "Friday" could not be more different from Crusoe—he's an unlettered "savage" who speaks a different language—yet they forge a real and caring relationship. In addition to its sheer reading pleasure as a survivalist tale, *Robinson Crusoe* presents a powerful narrative of the human need for other people. As chapter four presented, we are sacred in our individuality but also blessed in our need for other people.

Scriptural sources: The first reference in Scripture to our human need for other people is God's creation of Eve as a companion and helpmate to Adam: "It is not good for the man to be alone" (Genesis 2:18). The Tower of Babel story (Genesis 11:1–9) is a fascinating story about how challenging it is to successfully form community and work together for the common good. In one sense all the varied literature of the Bible is targeted toward teaching and cajoling people into living in harmony with one another.

This teaching is brought to perfection in the transcendent New Testament story of the Last Judgment in which Jesus teaches that in loving and meeting the needs of our neighbors we are loving Jesus himself (Matthew 25:31–46). Saint Paul teaches Christian understanding of human community through his writings on Eucharist and the

Christian community as the mystical body of Christ. The poor, the weak, the vulnerable among us are to be respected and cared for, and each of us is called to contribute our varied gifts for building up the whole community in truth and love (Ephesians 4; 1 Corinthians 12). The culminating biblical vision in the Book of Revelation (7:9–17) is people "from every nation, race, people, and tongue" gathered together entering fulfillment in the peace and joy of Christ's reign in heaven.

The Church's vision of community: In the Church's vision, the family is the necessary foundation of the ideal society in which every individual achieves fulfillment as a human being, and the common good—the good of the community as a whole—is also achieved. In a healthy family community we receive what we need to survive and grow from infancy to mature adulthood. Undoubtedly most of us remember how in family we learned our first lessons in respecting the rights and needs of others and we (hopefully) learned generosity and compassion toward others. From family we grow into larger communities of give and take—schools, jobs, and adult participation in the religious, civic, and governance activities of our particular culture. In contrast, American perspectives tend to define the individual as the basic "unit" of society.

An important aspect of community participation is having a meaningful voice in decisions that affect our lives. In the U.S. Catholic Bishops' letter on the American economy they stressed the right of public assistance recipients to have a voice in the services that they receive. Participation is simply another way to express support for democratic decision-making at all levels and sectors of society—church, workplace, local, and national government (*Economic Justice for All*, 1986, paragraph 78).

Government as an expression of community: The question of participation in decision-making brings us face-to-face with the increasingly contentious views among Americans concerning the proper role of government in society. Many Americans have an inherent distrust of government—after all we started out in rebellion against despotic government and in pioneer times people had to be quite hardy and self-sufficient. Yet even on the westward wide-open frontier, people quickly recognized the need to form government, churches, and other community groups to collectively meet their social and economic needs.

In Catholic teaching, government is a necessary and good feature of human society, not a necessary evil or even something to be "drowned in the bathtub" (done away with completely!). It is simply one important context in which we act together as a community to meet collective needs, protect the vulnerable, and foster the common good. Citizenship is a virtue, because through civic participation we keep government honest and working toward its true purpose: the U.S. Constitution identifies one of the major purposes of government as "to promote the general welfare"—namely the common good. True, as Christians, we can and should help through volunteerism and personal, charitable concern for others. However, the entire tradition of Catholic Social Teaching stresses that government is a necessary social institution that we ourselves create to work together toward justice and the orderly conduct of the whole society.

The word *subsidiarity* (related in meaning to subsidy or support) was first used by Pope Pius XI during the Great Depression to explain government's responsibility to actively support and assist families, and local organizations to thrive and do their job in society. (However, government may not take over their purposes or completely control them, as happened under Soviet communism). In the 2012 election campaign the U.S. Catholic Bishops publicly rejected the use of subsidiarity to justify massive cuts to programs that help people become independent and capable of contributing to society, such as college grants, Head Start, or food assistance. Clearly how much and what kind of government subsidies or supports are needed is a hotly contested question on which sincere people can legitimately disagree.

Nevertheless, to flatly demonize government or to imagine that justice and the common good can be achieved primarily through private or volunteer charitable efforts in a complex and large society is overly simplistic and certainly not in accord with the Church's traditional teaching on the purpose of government. It takes collective, democratic, and participatory good-faith efforts of everyone in a society to determine what kind and how much government action is appropriate to become a just society in which people are also free to live independently. Without informed, active citizens, governments trend toward either tyranny or plutocracy (rule by the rich and special interests), or just plain incompetence to respond adequately to large problems beyond the scope of local government or voluntary groups.

Searching for the common good: Catholic Social Teaching encourages us to express our faith and practice virtues, such as justice and prudence, through our exercise of active citizenship. How do we know if we are working for the common good and not just for our own individual or special group interests in our actions as citizens? To answer the question, consider this "thought experiment": Look at how an ideal happy family functions. Whether at home or on a family vacation, not everyone gets the exact same amount of anything (such as food or money) and not everyone has exactly the same decision-making power (parents have more say than children). But everyone's needs are met and everyone's varied interests are considered with respect—both family members and observers can see the happy results.

So too, in a society that strives for the common good everyone's basic needs are met and everyone's dignity and right to participate (in both work and public decision-making) is respected, taking into account variations in people's needs and their abilities to participate. Following Saint Augustine (*City of God*, Book 19, chapter 13), the Church stresses that good order in society must be based on just relationships among all people in that society (often translated as peace, stability, and security of a just order).

Dry as they are, when we read social statistics on problems such as unemployment, poverty, and crime rates and various measures of disease, violence, and unrest we can judge how far away or how close we are toward providing the material foundation to achieve the common good. In American society many of these negative social measures are rising (especially measures of poverty and economic inequality). As Catholics we are taught personal responsibility, but we also recognize the necessity of social responsibility to care for others, including through government provisions for human welfare. Love of neighbor is Christ's supreme command, but charitable giving alone cannot adequately ensure social justice and the common good.

The Catholic concept of the common good goes beyond the material basics of life. Our vision of a good society is one that actively fosters human flourishing: Every person has the means to develop his full humanity—skills and abilities yes, but also wholesome social, community roles, and relationships and freedom to grow morally and spiritually. The call to work for the common good permeates all of the social teaching documents of the Church.

The Church's teachings on community force us to think about the connections between our faith and our daily life in relationship to other people. As we reflect on our Christian vocation to work for the common good, let us ask ourselves honestly if our positions on public concerns, such as taxation, helping the poor and vulnerable, immigration, environmental protection, or any other contentious topic, are based primarily on "how will it affect me and my family and my business?" or if we also ask, "What public policy approach will help promote the goal of a just situation for all, especially for the poor and vulnerable?" We pray and work together to create the body of Christ, the communion of saints.

Psalms and Reflections

Psalm 133:1–3 (Poetic rejoicing in the delights of genuine community.)
Micah 4:1–4 (When we walk together in God's ways we shall experience universal peace and prosperity.)
James 3:13–18 (We must reject jealousy and ambition to achieve real wisdom, holiness, and peace among ourselves.)

The Documentary Heritage

—*Centesimus Annus* (*CA,* On the Hundredth Anniversary), John Paul II, 1991

In *CA,* the pope looks backward to review world events of the past one hundred years since publication of *Rerum Novarum*. He then assesses the current situation in the world in the light of the gospel and the basic values and principles in Catholic social justice teachings. John Paul II insists that social justice includes every single member of the human family, just as salvation is for all (paragraphs 51–54). The solutions to current social problems lie in cooperation, a commitment to the common good and society grounded in the "gift of grace"...."Grace, in cooperation with human freedom, constitutes that mysterious presence of God in history which is providence" (paragraph 58).

The past one hundred years have included the struggle for workers' rights, many very destructive wars, the positive efforts at development in the Third World, large technological changes, and more awareness of the importance of the natural world. People are also more aware of human ecology, most especially the need for strengthening family life.

In the wake of the fall of communism in eastern Europe, many feel that capitalism has triumphed. *CA* repeats the legitimacy of private property and its relationship to human dignity. Then Pope John Paul states the functions of the modern state (paragraphs 44 and 48), stressing the need for political control of markets, government's role to stabilize markets and financial systems and to provide public services the market cannot provide. Governments derive legitimacy from democratic participation, respect for human rights, and by observance of the principle of subsidiarity (supporting and strengthening local and intermediate level groups and organizations, especially family).

The Church also has a role in strengthening community and solidarity to prevent people's feeling lost and disconnected amid large-scale modern institutions of state and market (paragraph 49). The Church continues to speak out for the poor and for economic justice for all as essential to social justice and achievement of the universal common good. *CA* repeats the condemnation of war and insists that international development which enables the poor to achieve economic prosperity is the true way toward peace. Political solutions to today's challenges require cooperation and changes in economic and political power structures (paragraph 58).

After 100 years of social teachings, the Church still finds itself facing "new things," but the message continues to be a call to action, not just theory (paragraph 57).

Suggested Topics for Reflection and/or Discussion

1. Write down some ways in which you recognize your own interdependence—ways in which you receive things you need (material and nonmaterial)—through community with other people. (Consider family, friends, job, and your local, state, and national governments.)

2. How well do you think American society is doing at moving toward the common good, seen as "peace, stability, and the security of a just order"? How would you describe our progress? Consider both positive characteristics and areas of concern. Which groups or types of people are now most "left behind" in not sharing fully (equitably) in American well-being?

3. Summarize your understanding of what this chapter says about the Church's social teachings on the positive role of government in society. How does this contrast with a view of "the best government is that which governs least?" How does this contrast with a view that government is a necessary evil?

4. Reflect on what you already do, and, what more you might do, to be a responsible community member in your workplace or your local civic community? What does your parish or diocese do to teach about and promote the common good?

Action Step

This week I will....(for instance, pray, reflect on one of the scriptural passages to increase my appreciation for community; write a letter to my state and/or federal congressperson asking them to support improved services for a needy population, such as poor children, or unemployed people).

Closing Prayer

Repeat the opening prayer, sing a song, or pray a prayer of your own choosing.

CHAPTER SIX

Finding Holiness in the World: Work and Economic Life

Suggested Opening Song: "Lord of All Hopefulness" (*Gather Comprehensive Hymnal* #578) or "We Come to Share Our Story" (*Gather Comprehensive Hymnal* #613)

Opening Prayer:
God our Father,
by the labor of man [and woman] you govern and guide to perfection the work of creation.
Hear the prayers of your people
and give all [people] work that enhances their human dignity
and draws them closer to each other
in the service of their brothers [and sisters].
We ask this through our Lord Jesus Christ, your Son,
who lives and reigns with you and the Holy Spirit,
one God, forever and ever.

The Sacramentary, Prayers for Various Needs and Occasions,
#25 For the Blessings of Human Labor

Gospel Reading: Luke 12:22–34 (As we work to meet our daily needs, we are called to trust in Providence, resist anxiety, and put God's kingdom first in our concerns.)

Thematic Quote From Document:

Because Jesus' command to love our neighbor is universal, we hold that the life of each person on this globe is sacred. This commits us to bringing about a just economic order where all, without exception, will be treated with dignity and to working in collaboration with those who share this vision. The world is complex and this may often tempt us to seek simple and self-centered solutions; but as a community of disciples we are called to a new hope and a new vision that we must live without fear and without oversimplification.

ECONOMIC JUSTICE FOR ALL: PASTORAL LETTER
ON CATHOLIC SOCIAL TEACHING AND THE U.S. ECONOMY, 1986,
UNITED STATES CONFERENCE OF CATHOLIC BISHOPS, PAGE 163

Background Narrative

We sometimes joke about our mixed feelings around work—it seems like we "can't live with it, but can't live without it either!" Have you or a family member or a friend been unemployed for any significant period of time? If so, you know the suffering, anxiety, and economic peril that lack of work can bring. At the time of this writing, around nine percent of working-age people are experiencing either short- or long-term unemployment in the United States. Higher numbers persist in parts of Europe. If we include their families, then even more people suffer from unemployment. Chronic unemployment on Native American reservations approaches fifty to eighty percent in some places. In poor nations, 1.2 billion people constantly face starvation and death from lack of jobs and resources to secure the most basic necessities of life (such as water, food, shelter, and medical care).

Effects of unemployment: Work is a central need in the life of every adult. Research shows when people lack work that enables them to earn a living they experience stress so extreme it ranks with reactions to death and divorce. People deprived of meaningful work frequently experience significant physical and mental health problems, such as heart disease and suicidal thoughts, along with dire effects on their family life, such as substance abuse, violence, and divorce. Research, the daily news, and history show how large-scale unemployment and economic stress lead to disintegration of community life, sometimes to violence and war. Work, or the lack thereof, is related to all other aspects of living, including to our spiritual development—both as individuals and as communities of people.

Weighty questions of workplace justice: Numerous questions of justice arise within the workplace. Does the work pay enough to meet basic needs for housing, food, healthcare, and transportation? Does the work render a useful service or product to other people in society? Are the wages fair and equitable, in line with prevailing standards? Do the workers receive respect, security, reasonable hours, and the opportunity to develop their talents and skills? Do workers have a right to rest (a day off per week) and to annual days of leave for family and personal renewal? Do they participate in decisions about how the enterprise is managed and how the job should be done, or are they expected to simply "follow orders?" Whose duty is it to ensure that these questions and others about work can be answered affirmatively? What is the responsibility of the individual, the government and private economic enterprises for ensuring useful work for all, with fair wages and working conditions? These are just a few of the weighty questions about workplace justice and meaning.

Major Church documents on work: The subject of work, addressing questions raised above, has been a leading theme in the development of modern Catholic social-justice teachings. Pope Leo XIII's encyclical *Rerum Novarum* (On Capital and Labor, 1891) spelled out some basic justice principles and standards for treatment of workers in the industrial system of Europe and America. Catholic working-class people and their advocates were greatly heartened in their struggles for workplace justice by this initial Vatican teaching about the moral and spiritual meaning of work and modern economic systems.

For a century, Catholic Social Teaching on human work developed in the context of the larger global struggle between communism and capitalism as models for how to run modern economies and what the role of government should be in the economic life of nations. Several more recent notable documents that address work and economic life include *Laborem Exercens* (On Human Work, 1981); *Centesimus Annus* (On the Hundredth Anniversary of *Rerum Novarum*, 1991); encyclicals by Pope John Paul II; and the 1986 pastoral letter of the U.S. Conference of Catholic Bishops, quoted above.

Scriptural sources: In the beginning of Scripture (Genesis, chapters 1–4) work is presented with several features:

- Human work has **dignity** because we ourselves are God's work, created in the image of God.
- Work expresses divine **creativity**. In doing good work we share in God's ongoing creative action in the universe: whether growing a garden, raising a child, teaching, healing, or producing other wholesome goods and services.
- Through work we carry out God's command to be **responsible stewards** in the way we use and cherish plants, animals, and other goods of the earth (water, air, land, minerals).
- Following the sin and expulsion of Adam and Eve from Eden, and Cain's murder of Abel, work also appears as a **punishment**—a hard task with suffering and indignity, imposed by human sin and disobedience.

No doubt the Genesis author(s) struggled with the very same paradox that we all experience about work: sometimes it feels like a blessing and sometimes like a curse! The prophets speak constantly about work: They focus on the social justice aspects of work, condemning the behavior of those who claim to worship the true God, while actively conspiring to defraud workers of their just wages, or poor farmers of just prices for their products (see Isaiah 58; Amos 5:10–15; Psalm 10, Psalm 37).

Jesus' life as a carpenter—and his teaching and healing ministry—enhances the meaning about the dignity of human work and helps us see our own occupations as a "calling"—a vocation from God. From the life of Jesus and the teachings of Saint Paul, we learn that through work we share in God's creative work, and, amazingly, in God's redemptive work for all humanity. Work is one of the most significant ways in which we serve our neighbors and fulfill our own spiritual calling to love others as we cherish ourselves.

Rights and responsibilities in the workplace: Catholic Social Teachings spell out some of the concrete provisions needed to ensure the dignity and the justice of human work. John Paul II in particular stresses that even so-called menial work has dignity because the one doing the work—a human person—has dignity. Karol Wojtyla (John Paul II) experienced menial and hard forced labor under the Nazis in a stone quarry during World War II. He also experienced the effects on whole societies from the distortions in work structures under the Soviet communist system. While contemporary work frequently involves an employer-employee relationship, the work of raising a family, volunteering, or doing creative, artistic work also contributes worthily to human good and deserves respect and societal support. For example, parents who stay at home to raise children might be included in policies for tax-supported retirement and disability benefits, to demonstrate our recognition of the importance of child-rearing as good work for society.

As noted in earlier chapters, people have rights to the basic necessities of life, a right to a balance between work and other areas of human life, the right to associate with others for common purpose, the right to have a meaningful voice in decisions that affect one's own situation, a right to dignity in old age. It follows that to honor these rights, workers need living wages (including old-age security), a reasonable balance between required hours of work, and time for leisure (time for family, worship, and recreation).

To secure these rights, workers may justly form unions to represent them in workplace negotiations. In contrast to prevailing practice in many capitalist workplaces, as well as in the defunct communist system, the Church also supports real worker participation in management decision-making in the workplace, especially if the decisions directly impact the workers themselves. A living example of workplaces modeled on Catholic Social Teachings about worker participation is the Mondragon cooperative system in the Basque region of Spain. These successful industrial cooperative businesses were started after World War II by five young men studying Church Social Teachings with their parish priest.

Workers' rights are balanced with their responsibilities to work honestly and industriously for their wages and to temper their demands for changes in wages or working conditions with judicious concern for the common good of the whole community. Employers also have duties to balance the goal of profit with the well-being of their employees and to consider how their business activities affect progress toward achieving the common good.

Economic systems and public policy: Catholic Social Teaching asserts that government also has proactive duties with regard to work and economic conditions in society. Government should promote policies and programs that foster employment and protect the rights of workers, including their right to form unions.

While communism prevailed in eastern Europe, the Church strongly criticized the totalitarian effort of communist governments to control all of society. In more recent years, Church teachings have paid more attention to the excesses of capitalism when government fails to regulate business to ensure fairness and transparency in how it operates. (A great portion of the recent "meltdown" in investment banking can be traced, without political prejudice, to weak regulatory policies.) Church teaching acknowledges positive aspects of capitalism, such as encouragement of creativity and hard work. However, the sinful results of capitalism are also pointed out: uncontrolled greed, increasing economic inequality and consumerism, millions left behind with no jobs or adequate income, unfair profits, manipulation of international trade to the advantage of large corporations and richer nations, and the use of earth's resources in destructive, unsustainable patterns. Pope Benedict XVI's encyclical *Caritas in Veritate* (Charity in Truth, 2009) discusses how the Christian virtues of charity and truth can and should govern secular economic activity.

In short, economic justice requires that we pay attention to national and even international levels of public policies and programs. The Center of Concern, a Catholic think tank in Washington, D.C., is a good source for learning more about advocacy for international economic justice (see Appendix B). It is the moral duty of Catholic laity—both employers and employees—to understand the basic justice teachings of the Church and to use their personal knowledge and skills to work for their application in their own work settings and in the economic policies of government. At work we achieve holiness through living in charity, truth, and justice. Through good (just) work we become "the salt of the earth (and) the light of the world" (Matthew 5:13–14).

Psalms and Reflections

Psalm 37:1–4, 7–14c, 16–19 (Those who trust God and work with integrity will be protected and dwell in God's peace.)

Isaiah 58:3–4 (True worship requires freedom from oppression, justice for workers, and concern for the poor.)

Matthew 12:33–37 (Do we bring forth good or evil fruits from our work?)

1 Timothy 5:17–19 (God's economy calls for sharing our wealth and doing good for others.)

The Documentary Heritage

—*Economic Justice for All*, United States Conference of Catholic Bishops, 1986

In this pastoral letter, the American bishops begin with a brief review of then-current urgent concerns in the functioning of the economy, such as global competition and "stark inequities across countries" (page 7), depletion of natural resources, high rates of unemployment and poverty, and the effects of these economic problems on families and communities. They declare their intention to draw attention to the social justice aspects of these and other economic issues (chapter 1).

In chapter 2 the moral and religious aspects of economic activity are spelled out, drawing on both biblical perspectives and concepts from the Catholic tradition. Most basically, economic institutions must serve and respect the human dignity of the person. Because we are created in God's image, our work is a share in God's creative work. We are called to serve others as we would serve Christ, to form community, and see our work as a participation in building up the reign (kingdom) of God. Scripture provides strong warnings against the dangers of wealth and the obligation to consider the poor.

Ethical norms discussed include:

- (A) the duty to promote community, solidarity, and even love in the economic realm.
- (B) fairness in contracts and exchange (commutative justice); in this context the letter states that productivity and profit must be weighed in relationship to issues of discrimination, environmental impacts, and workers' ability to meet their basic needs (adequate wages) (page 37).
- (C) distributive justice, which is defined as "the allocation of income, wealth, and power in society...evaluated in light of its effects on persons whose basic material needs are unmet" (page 36). The United States is not so poor that people's basic needs cannot be met. While personal greed and materialism are discouraged, more attention is needed by the government and other social institutions to ensure that unjust distribution of power and wealth is reduced.
- (D) overcoming the marginalization and powerlessness of poverty. Greater opportunities for participation are needed, including political/civil rights as well as economic rights (jobs, property, etc.).

The bishops call upon citizens to make an "option for the poor" an economic priority for the nation. They spell out explicitly that this priority includes meeting basic needs, improving access to employment, and directing resources of "wealth, talent, and human energy" (page 47) toward reducing poverty and strengthening family life. Boldly, they state the contrast to policies that prioritize luxury goods and military technology (page 48).

The pastoral letter goes on to discuss the responsibilities of labor (particularly labor unions), the duties of owners and managers, and the role of citizens and government in creating a more just and equitable economy. In addition to poverty and unemployment, the letter also addresses specific concerns in the field of food and agriculture, and it calls for greater fairness and cooperation in relationship to developing nations.

A "New American Experiment" (page 145) is called for to increase cooperative efforts in economic enterprises at local, regional, national, and international levels. The letter concludes with a meditation on the role of the Church as a whole and of individuals in the Christian duty to promote justice and charity in the marketplace. The bishops acknowledge the duty of the Church itself to practice justice as an employer. We are called to "holiness in the world," through the way we live our economic lives (page 167).

Suggested Topics for Reflection and/or Discussion

1. Read aloud a sentence or paragraph from this chapter that most helped you reach a new understanding of the religious or moral meaning of human work.

2. How do you think about the meaning and purpose of your own work? How has this chapter helped you see the moral and spiritual dimensions of your own work in a new way?

3. How has the discussion on the Church's teachings about work and economic justice influenced your thinking about unemployment? After reading this chapter, would you agree that government has some responsibility for ensuring employment for all?

4. Some Americans believe that "unions are no longer needed" because the problems they worked on have all been solved. Explain why you agree or disagree with this statement. What is your response to the Church's teaching that unions in the workplace are important to promote community and human solidarity, not just better financial returns for workers?

5. The Church's vision is that a just economic system should meet the basic needs of everyone, provide employment for all, diminish discrimination, protect the environment, and build a sense of community. Based on these criteria, what kind of "grade" would you give the U.S. economy today? The world economy? Succeeding well? Failing miserably? Somewhere in between? Explain your grade.

Action Step

This week I will....(for instance, examine my conscience to see what changes in attitude or behavior I might need on my own work; write a letter to the editor in favor of better public efforts to support job creation).

Closing Prayer

Repeat the opening prayer, sing a song, or pray a prayer of your own choosing.

CHAPTER SEVEN

Globalization and Its Discontents: One Human Family or Just One Big Global Mall?

Suggested Opening Song: "In Christ There Is No East or West" (*Gather Comprehensive Hymnal* #738) or "All Are Welcome" (*Gather Comprehensive Hymnal* #753)

Opening Prayer:
Father,
you have given all peoples one common origin,
and your will is to gather them as one family in yourself.
Fill the hearts of all [people] with the fire of your love
and the desire to ensure justice for all their brothers and sisters.
By sharing the good things you give us
may we secure justice and equality for every human being,
an end to all division
and a human society built on love and peace.
We ask this through our Lord Jesus Christ, your Son,
who lives and reigns with you and the Holy Spirit,
one God, forever and ever.

The Sacramentary, Prayers for Various Needs and Occasions,
#21 For the Progress of Peoples

Gospel Reading: Matthew 25:31–46 (Our service to those in need is direct service to Christ. At the Last Judgment we will be judged on how we treated the least among us.)

Thematic Quote From Document:

> *The struggle against destitution, though urgent and necessary, is not enough. It is a question, rather, of building a world where every man, no matter what his race, religion or nationality, can live a fully human life, freed from servitude imposed on him by other men or by natural forces over which he has not sufficient control; a world where freedom is not an empty word and where the poor man Lazarus can sit down at the same table with the rich man. This demands great generosity, much sacrifice and unceasing effort on the part of the rich man* (paragraph 47).
>
> POPULORUM PROGRESSIO
(ON THE DEVELOPMENT OF PEOPLES), PAUL VI, 1967

Background Narrative

During the American Revolution, the leaders were quarreling among themselves over how to proceed. Benjamin Franklin warned, "We must all hang together, or assuredly we shall all hang separately" (meaning they'd hang as traitors to King George). This pithy bit of folk wisdom surely applies to the entire global human family now more than ever before. We will thrive as a human family only if we can find ways to work together to meet many current global challenges, such as poverty, disease, migration, climate change, and violence.

During the twentieth century, forces such as World War II, the advent of air travel, and, most recently, the electronic communication revolution have hastened and intensified the commercial and financial relationships among nations and regions—the phenomenon we call "globalization." The Church's vision of international human solidarity far transcends commercial exchange. As presented in chapter five, in the eyes of God we are all one human family, related and responsible to one another. The Christian virtue of solidarity is particularly linked to our care and concern for the poor and vulnerable, whether within our own country or in poor nations around the globe.

Scriptural sources: Our responsibility for one another is first raised in Genesis 4:1–16, where we hear the angry cry of Cain—"Am I my brother's keeper?" God's answer is a most definite, "Yes you are!" Many Old Testament stories demonstrate the Jewish people's increasing understanding that God's compassion and care are for all people. A few of the most powerful stories are the story of Abraham's hospitality to strangers (Genesis 18:1–10), Ruth's blessed faithfulness (she was a non-Jewish ancestor of Jesus), the story of Naaman, a foreign army commander healed from leprosy through the prophet Elisha (2 Kings 5:1–14). As well, the many decrees given by Moses and the later prophets insist the justification of the Jewish people before God is dependent on how they treat the poor and vulnerable, the alien and stranger among them: "[God] executes justice for the orphan and the widow, and loves the resident alien, giving them food and clothing. So you too should love the resident alien...for that is what you were in the land of Egypt" (Deuteronomy 10:18–19).

Jesus also taught by story, command, and example that God's concern extends to all people: the healing of the Roman centurion's servant (Luke 7:1–10), the healing of the daughter of a foreign (Syrophoenician) woman (Mark 7:24–30); his marvelous dialogue of hope for salvation with the Samaritan woman at the well (John 4:5–30). Through the parable of the Good Samaritan (Luke 10:29–37), Jesus showed us our neighbor is anyone we encounter in need of help. Most importantly, as our Last Judgment reading reveals, at death we will be judged on how we treated the "least" among us—the poor, hungry, sick, and imprisoned.

In the Acts of the Apostles chapter 10, while Saint Peter sojourned with Cornelius the Roman centurion, he had a fantastic vision from which he learned the saving good news of the resurrected Christ was for all people. Other New Testament sources which point to the universality of God's love include the journey of the Magi (pagan wise men) to worship the infant Jesus, the first Pentecost outpouring of the Holy Spirit upon people of many nations, the cosmic vision of Revelation in which people from all nations come in procession to worship before the throne of the Lamb (see Revelation 5:9–10; 7:9–10; 21:24–25).

The meaning of solidarity: The term "solidarity" came into vogue during the 1980s with the Polish workers' revolt against the Communist regime, led by Lech Walesa. Pope John Paul II gave moral and political support to the workers' movement for justice that ultimately helped bring about the collapse of Communist rule in eastern European countries. In his writings, (especially *Sollicitudo Rei Socialis* [On Social Concerns], 1987) Pope John Paul helped expand the meaning of solidarity as a Christian virtue signifying our actions to respect the integral unity of the human family.

Global solidarity requires, first and foremost, concern for the poor. Church leaders from Europe and America gained greater awareness and concern regarding global poverty from the participation of so many bishops from poor nations at the Second Vatican Council. The council document *Gaudium et Spes*, discussed in chapter one, grew from increased awareness that Catholicism is truly a global Church.

Solidarity contains a distinctive view of development: In his 1967 encyclical *Populorum Progressio* (*PP*, On the Development of Peoples), Paul VI draws out the relationships between development and peace; and he stresses the moral duty of wealthier nations to help improve human development conditions in poor societies (what used to be called "the Third World"). In contrast to purely economic and pragmatic analysis, Catholic Social Teaching stresses that development—poverty alleviation—must consider and respect the whole person, including people's spiritual needs and their social/cultural heritage. Large-scale economic projects alone do not comprise human social development. Fortunately, many Catholic organizations, such as Catholic Relief Services, set an excellent example of how to assist poor communities in such an integral manner (see Appendix B).

International cooperation for human development: World War II and the Cold War also heightened people's understanding of the connections among poverty, human development, and peace within and between nations. Through the United Nations and its various agencies, the world community has made some progress in measuring poverty and its attendant ills. Though great poverty remains, we have made significant strides in reducing poverty in many countries and regions of the world. Much of this success is based on two key components of action:

(1) involve poor people themselves in leadership and action to improve their lives, and,

(2) achieve cooperation among the United Nations, national governments, nongovernmental development groups, and many religious groups, including many Catholic organizations. This is the kind of cooperation that John Paul II called for in *Centesimus Annus* (1991).

Since the year 2000, under the aegis of the United Nations, the Millennium Development Goals (un.org/millenniumgoals) have given us concrete, measurable goals such as universal education, equality for women, improvement in child and maternal health, reductions in infectious disease, environmental sustainability, and improved global partnerships for action (between both governmental and voluntary groups). Still, global poverty and global inequality remain stark: the world's poorest forty percent have only five percent of global income; every day 22,000 or more children die from poverty-related causes (hunger and disease); millions of people live in slums, lacking secure access to the most basic of needs—food, clean water, sanitation, and electricity (*Poverty Facts and Stats*, 2012).

Economic policies, environmental disasters, and violent conflicts contribute to the large numbers of refugees and migrant populations, surely the poorest people in the world, estimated by the United Nations agency for refugees at possibly up to forty-two million displaced persons (unhcr.org).

Charity and justice response to global poverty: Surely we must pause to consider the profound human suffering behind these terrible statistical measures. Catholic social-justice teachings on solidarity and concern for the poor plead for a change of heart on the part of the well-to-do—that we honestly confront the moral implications of how our own affluence and consumerism affects other people, even though they live far away.

Church teaching also consistently stresses needed changes in national and international institutions, such as trade and monetary policies that unfairly benefit the wealthy. In the Catholic approach to social justice, meeting everyone's basic needs is the first purpose of any economy before the creation of wealth. For example, consumerism and trade policy come together in everyday products like coffee, chocolate, and cut flowers: Land that could be used by local people to grow their own food is diverted to grow luxury products for export because of market forces. Many churches now sell Fair Trade Coffee as a modest solidarity measure to at least ensure that peasant coffee growers receive fair prices.

Most importantly, as papal teaching consistently asserts, the poor cannot be simply passive recipients of endless emergency relief campaigns or economic development schemes imported and imposed by powerful international aid and development agencies. Disadvantaged communities and nations must experience participatory justice. They must obtain political power and economic resources to participate in finding effective and secure ways to meet their own material needs and to achieve their full human social and spiritual development. Countries cannot all be run in exactly the same way, but people everywhere have basic justice rights, free from internal tyranny and violence as well as from excessive international economic inequities imposed by stronger nations.

How does one person or one parish family become a part of global development to express our Christian commitment to solidarity? Do not try to do it alone! Suggestions are presented in Appendix A, and Church resource organizations are listed in Appendix B. Learning and action can commence with individual and local parish participation with numerous existing Catholic organizations. Start anywhere: No matter which specific issue or need you attempt to respond to, you will learn about the causes of global poverty, and you will gradually gain a larger picture of our deep solidarity with the entire human family.

Psalms and Reflections

Psalm 67:1–5 (We pray for God's blessings on all people and nations.)
Genesis 4:1–8 (Cain is held responsible for his brother Abel's death.)
Isaiah 58:1–12 (True penance and acceptable worship desired by God is
  for justice for the poor, and freedom from oppression for all people.)
Acts 10:34–35 (God does not have favorite peoples or nations. The
  Good News of peace is for all people: Jesus Christ is Lord of all.)

The Documentary Heritage

—*Populorum Progressio* (*PP*, On the Development of Peoples), Pope
Paul VI, 1967

This encyclical concludes by asking "...if the new name of peace is
development, who would not want to work toward its achievement
with all his powers" (paragraph 87). Paul VI had traveled to countries
in South America, Africa, and Asia and so had observed conditions
of dire poverty firsthand. This personal experience in what used to
be called the "Third World" influenced his great concern with the
urgency of development for these regions of the world. He departed
from existing ideas and practices of development by considering the
human moral and political challenges, not merely economic measures
of development (Deck, 2004). The end result Paul VI envisioned is a
world in which every person can lead a more truly human life "loved
and helped as his brother, as his neighbor" (paragraph 82).

Four levels of human development are: (A) freedom from exploita-
tion due to inequities in power and wealth; (B) access to a decent level
of material necessities as well as education and cultural resources;
(C) increased capacity to respect other people's human dignity, seek
peace and the common good; and (D) acquisition of values and faith
in God (paragraph 21).

Paul VI acknowledges the struggles of the poor for a better life—in
fact they have a duty to work for their own development. While he
recognizes the extreme inequities in political power that maintain

such economic and social inequities, he encourages reform and not revolution. He decries violence as it usually makes things worse, but, under conditions of extreme tyranny, such action sometimes occurs (paragraph 31).

PP credits Catholic missionary efforts to meet people's human needs through establishing schools and hospitals and other needed services in poor nations, but world conditions call for larger, more coordinated international efforts. The encyclical reviews the obligations of wealthy nations to help the poorer, insisting that both will be better off as a result. Trade relationships require regulation to ensure fairness to the weaker partners (paragraphs 56–61). World-level coordinated planning and establishment of a "World Fund" for the "most destitute" are called for (paragraph 51). This is the nature of human solidarity.

PP strongly denounces the arms race, as such funds could be used to help with development of schools, hospitals, and homes. Excessive nationalism, racism, and inhuman conditions for emigrant workers are noted, and Paul VI bluntly declares, "The world is sick" (paragraph 66). Industrialism in itself is not wrong; the fault lies in unregulated capitalism, where the profit motive reigns supreme. Repeatedly, the encyclical confirms that true development is not just economic betterment but requires the full, integral development of the human being.

Populorum Progressio is a strong document. It encourages human solidarity, instructs wealthy nations in their duties toward the poor, explains that development encompasses the whole person in cultural context, and argues that development leads to world peace. Theologian Allan Figueroa Deck states that *PP* had a strong influence on the rise of small (base) Christian communities in Latin America, Africa, and Asia, which made "one of the more original, extensive and influential applications of Catholic Social Teaching ever achieved" (Deck, 2004, page 310).

Additional Reading on Development

—*Sollicitudo Rei Socialis* (On Social Concerns), Pope John Paul II, 1987

Suggested Topics for Reflection and Discussion

1. What experiences and relationships have you had with people culturally "different" from yourself, (whether in your local community or through volunteerism, work, and travel in other areas of the country or world). What does your experience mean to you? How have your experiences and relationships influenced your beliefs, values, and actions?

2. The Church's teachings on solidarity and our duties to the poor stress that both "hearts" (individual attitudes and behaviors) and political/economic institutions (laws and policies) must change. Do you agree with this twofold perspective? Why or why not? Can you think of some examples of situations where both "hearts and institutions" have changed to make a positive difference in people's lives? Some examples to consider from our own society might include racial discrimination, abuse of women and children, or the treatment of immigrants.

3. Based on Matthew's Gospel description of the Last Judgment (Matthew 25:31–46), consider some ways you and your parish could practice both charitable and justice response to world poverty. For example, start a Fair Trade Coffee and Tea sales program with Catholic Relief Services (CRS), and learn how you and your parish can cooperate with CRS and the United States Conference of Catholic Bishops on advocacy for international justice concerns.

4. What other idea or perspective about human solidarity did you most appreciate from this chapter's reading?

Action Step

This week I will....(for instance, research Catholic Relief Services or another international aid group on the Internet; study the action ideas in Appendix A and choose one idea to pledge to work on).

Closing Prayer

Repeat the opening prayer, sing a song, or pray a prayer of your own choosing.

CHAPTER EIGHT

All My Relations: Spiritual and Moral Dimensions of Creation Care

Suggested Opening Song: "For the Beauty of the Earth" (*Gather Comprehensive Hymnal* #572) or "Canticle of the Sun" (*Gather Comprehensive Hymnal* #496)

Opening Prayer:
Let us pray [for the faith to recognize God's presence in our world]

Pause for silent prayer

God our Father,
open our eyes to see your hand at work
in the splendor of creation,
in the beauty of human life.
Touched by your hand our world is holy.
Help us to cherish the gifts that surround us,
to share your blessings with our brothers and sisters,
and to experience the joy of life in your presence.
We ask this through Christ our Lord.

The Sacramentary, Alternative Opening Prayer,
Seventeenth Sunday in Ordinary Time

Gospel Prayer: Luke 12:16–21 (We are called to self-restraint in our quest for wealth and material comfort. Our true treasure is spiritual.)

Thematic Quote From Document:

> *When the ecological crisis is set within the broader context of the* **search for peace** *within society, we can understand better the importance of giving attention to what the earth and its atmosphere are telling us: namely, that there is an order in the universe which must be respected, and the human person, endowed with the capability of choosing freely, has a grave responsibility to preserve this order for the well-being of future generations. I wish to repeat that* **the ecological crisis is a moral issue**.

PEACE WITH GOD THE CREATOR, PEACE WITH ALL OF CREATION,
WORLD DAY OF PEACE MESSAGE, POPE JOHN PAUL II,
JANUARY 1, 1990, SECTION V

Background Narrative

Today, people are more aware of the stupendous beauty and mysterious riches of creation, thanks to education, scientific advances and our greater opportunity to travel and experience the wonderfully varied regions of the earth. As we receive new astronomical knowledge of the immensity of the universe—as well as expanding scientific knowledge about life on earth—we are drawn to awe and greater humility about ourselves as human beings in this complex universe—a universe that goes on being created by the holy mystery whom we call God. As Fyodor Dostoevsky said (in the person of Father Zossima in *The Brothers Karamazov*):

"Love all God's creation, the whole and every grain of sand in it. Love every leaf, every ray of God's, light. Love the animals, love the plants, love everything. If you love everything, you will perceive the divine mystery in things...And you will come at last to love the whole world with an all-embracing love" (Dostoevsky, 1952, page 167).

All My Relations: In Catholic Social Teaching all creation is about relationships of love. These include:

- God's relationship to all that exists, as Creator, Savior, and life-giving Spirit (the Trinity)

- Our relationship as humans to each other and to all other created things (animals, plants, land, water, sky, and all else in the universe)
- Our relationship to God as enlivened through our experiences of other created things.

My friend Mary Kay told me how her father used to take her to their farm fields to scoop up and feel the richness of the soil. He explained to her how God gave his sacred power to provide food and they were to be grateful. He understood the Catholic ability to see the holiness of nature's gifts. Our sacramental traditions provide us with rich resources for constantly remembering the sacred connections among nature, human life, and God. Our sacred rituals of sacraments and prayers through the Church year use the basic elements of the earth—water, oil from plants, dust of the earth, palm branches, fire and wind, colors, the seasons of the year, references to sun, moon and stars, flowers, even bees and honey.

A call to help suffering creation: The call to environmental responsibility expands the message of justice to all of creation. "As the Church itself is called to conversion to the side of the poor in the struggle of justice and to the side of women in their struggle for full equality, so the Church itself is called to conversion to the side of suffering creation" (Edwards, 2006, page 3). John Paul II has also noted that creation is suffering (*Peace With God the Creator*, 1990).

If we are willing to risk developing empathy for the suffering of creation (including the sufferings of people who live in horribly degraded and depleted local environments) we can rise to a new level of Christian compassion and sorrow for our collective excesses and lack of respect for creation. In addition to passion for justice, such reflection should lead us to practice many other virtues in how we use earth's resources, such as self-discipline, generosity, simplicity of lifestyle, humility, gratitude, and joy in life itself. In this way we can realize Jesus' promise: Through dying to self (selfishness and greed), we will rise to new life (see Matthew 16:24–26).

Church leaders address environmental concerns: Basic Catholic beliefs and social-justice values and principles discussed throughout this book apply to environmental problems. John Paul II and Benedict XVI have stressed environmental responsibility as a moral issue, grounded in a profound respect for all of life. The first Vatican statement to explicitly address the moral and religious dimensions of environmental concerns was Pope John Paul II's message for World Day of Peace quoted above. Pope Benedict XVI and bishops in various nations and regions around the globe have also urged more responsible action on environmental problems. For example, the U.S. and Canadian bishops of the Pacific Northwest issued a statement on the Columbia River (The Columbia River Watershed, 2001). The U.S. Conference of Catholic Bishops (USCCB) has issued documents on global climate change and teaching materials for parish study groups, and it also participates in the national Interreligious Partnership for the Environment. The USCCB and other Catholic advocacy groups also issue messages to government, such as a message to the Environmental Protection Agency, pointing out that mercury pollution from power plants threatens the lives of born and unborn children, as well as other poor and vulnerable groups (Catholic Coalition on Climate Change, Weekly Update, June 22, 2011). The National Catholic Rural Life Conference (NCRLC) sponsors the Catholic Coalition on Climate Change, as well as advocacy for safe food and justice for family farmers.

Practical action at the local level: Numerous other groups, including parishes and academic specialists, work to expand understanding of the relationships between religious belief and our responsibility to protect and cherish the earth. Catholic and Protestant churches around the country have implemented some admirable practices:

- installing better energy efficiency resources in their buildings such as solar panels or improved insulation (which also saves parishes money);
- planting gardens and orchards in place of lawns (thus providing food for both members and local food banks);

- replacing throw-away dining supplies with reusable dishes;
- sponsoring Fair Trade markets (such as coffee and other products from Catholic Relief Services) to advance economic justice for poor farmers;
- developing teaching materials to help their members practice better environmental stewardship in their homes and providing advocacy education for environmental justice for farm workers or for better safety precautions around herbicides and pesticides used in food production (See National Catholic Rural Life Conference, Appendix B);
- sponsoring prayer services with an ecological theme such as blessing animals or adapting the traditional Catholic "rogation days" of prayer for rain to pray for a larger range of current environmental concerns;
- participating in local civic environmental services such as volunteer restoration of a stream bed, cleaning up a littered roadway, park, or abused beach.

Environmental justice is social justice: Environmental practices have serious implications for justice to individuals as well as for social justice and the common good. Farm workers and poor people in rural and urban areas suffer diseases resulting from exposure to high levels of dangerous substances from agriculture, industry, and waste disposal sites, and many lack necessary good environmental resources (such as clean water, safe food, decent housing, etc.). In the Bronx (New York), the majority of children have asthma, related to high concentrations of dangerous industrial toxins.

International trade, driven by unfettered profit-seeking and unequal bargaining power, undermines human solidarity and disregards the "option for the poor" as poorer nations produce goods for export, rather than for the needs of their own people. The Church's persistent demand for fairness in international economic exchange now includes recognition of the serious environmental impacts of current patterns. For example, the earth's "lungs," the Amazon rainforest is being cut down at alarming rates to raise beef, soy, and other products for the international market. Sister Dorothy Stang, murdered in 2005, combined her advocacy for the rights of the peasants with efforts to protect the rainforest they desperately depend on for life (See Appendix C).

John Paul II identified excessive consumerism, "indiscriminate application of advances in science and technology" (*Peace With God the Creator* 1990, section II), and human-caused global climate change as major features of today's environmental crisis. He noted their threat to intergenerational justice—the fate of our grandchildren. God gave us the earth in stewardship and we must pay attention to "the well-being of future generations" (ibid., section II). John Paul II and Benedict XVI have also noted how war and armed conflict destroys natural resources in addition to destroying people.

Basic Catholic beliefs embedded in creation: God's very nature as Trinity is relational and dynamic, and this includes how God *continually* relates to all of creation with infinite love. The Trinity is expressed and reflected in the relationships and dynamism of all creation. Science confirms our Christian belief that creation mirrors and participates in dynamic relationship with God: Einstein reportedly said the foundational principle of science is that "everything is related to everything." Understanding this encourages humility and caution about our over-reliance on technologies that interfere with the complex relationships in ecosystems. Examples include exterminating entire species or introducing foreign species into local ecosystems or altering entire local environments through vast engineering projects such as dams. Studying and honoring how plants, animals and wind, soil and water on earth relate to one another can lead us to a deeper appreciation of how we find God in our relationships to all creation.

We believe all creation, all life, is sacred; all creation is redeemed, transformed and fulfilled by the Incarnation of God among us in the person of Jesus (Romans 8:18–23). How can we cherish human life without also understanding that other living creatures also have a real beauty, dignity, and purpose of their own in God's plan for creation? Saint Thomas Aquinas taught that every creature reveals something about the beauty, goodness, and truth of God. The bishops have insisted —we must respect the *integrity* of creation—use the resources we need to foster human life respectfully and prudently, without destroying the ability of plants, animals, and natural systems (rivers, oceans, prairies, weather patterns, etc.) to also function in their own natural way (*Global Climate Change*, 2001). Recall that prudence (good judgment) is one of the four basic (cardinal) virtues in Catholic theology. It seems a virtue urgently needed to address serious environmental problems in the world today.

The life and teachings of Jesus draw us to a life of generosity, simplicity, compassion for others, trust in God's abundance to supply our needs, self-denial for the sake of respecting creation's limits, and serving others to bring about the realization of God's reign of justice and love. The death and resurrection of Jesus along with the Spirit of Pentecost, commissioning the disciples to go forth to spread the Good News of God's creative presence among us, demonstrate that life and hope, meaning and purpose flow from what kind of persons we become, not from how much "stuff" we accumulate. Genuine practice of Christian virtues will inevitably lead us to greater thoughtfulness and moderation in how we use the goods of creation and to a human life that is truly alive!

These basic Christian beliefs and virtue practices can help us toward more thoughtful, temperate use of created goods and so help us reach out to benefit the poor of our world who do not have enough to sustain a life of human dignity and fulfillment. If we take more time to experience the beauty and mystery of nature firsthand—and bring the children along away from their electronic toys—we will undoubtedly deepen our appreciation and gratitude toward God and of Pentecost: "Send forth your spirit, they are created and you renew the face of the earth. May the glory of the LORD endure forever; may the LORD be glad in his works!" (Psalm 104:30–31).

Psalms and Scriptural Reflections

Psalm 104 (A beautiful meditation on God's intimate presence in the natural world.)

Genesis 1:1–2, 31; 2:1–3 (Everything that God has made is "very good.")

Luke 8:24–25 (Christ is master of the wind and the waves; we trust in him.)

Romans 8:18–23 (ALL creation participates in the glory and hope of freedom from death and decay.)

Revelation 21:1–6 (Christ is the beginning and the goal of all that exists: God's saving action makes all of creation new and overcomes suffering and death.)

The Documentary Heritage

—*Peace With God the Creator, Peace With All of Creation*, World Day of Peace Message, Pope John Paul II, January 1, 1990

This message was the first papal pronouncement devoted primarily to ecological concerns. John Paul II draws out the relationships between "a new **ecological awareness**" and "the **development of a peaceful society**" (Introduction). The message begins by reviewing the basic biblical beliefs and teachings that support our respect for creation: the goodness of creation and the reconciliation of "**all things**" (section 1) in Christ, not only humanity. While modern science and technology have brought great benefits, it is now very apparent that their application to industry and agriculture have raised profound moral questions and have even caused great harm. Observance of ethical norms, notably respect for life and ecological integrity are essential to bringing about a peaceful society (section 2).

Several essential components of a solution to restoring creation include:

(A) Accepting the truth that earth's resources are intended by God for the good of all; the terrible imbalance between the rich and poor are "manifestly unjust" (section 3). Those who are more well-off must assess the ecological costs of consumerist lifestyles (section 4).

(B) "A more internationally coordinated approach to the management of the earth's goods" (sections 3 and 4).

(C) A responsibility for nations to see a safe environment as a basic human right, taking special care for the more vulnerable members of their society (section 3).

(D) Social and economic reforms are needed to relieve poverty, which contributes to ecological destruction, such as rural land reform and debt relief (section 4).

(E) War causes much ecological damage. John Paul calls for "education in ecological responsibility" an increase in appreciation for the "aesthetic value of creation" and a new sense of urgency that everyone has responsibility to respond to the moral dimensions of "the ecological crisis" (section 5). He concludes by emphasizing the particular obligations of Catholics to care for creation as part of our respect for life and human dignity.

Additional Reading

—*Global Climate Change: a Plea for Dialogue, Prudence and the Common Good.* A statement of the U.S. Catholic Bishops, USCCB, 2001

—*Caritas in Veritate* (Charity in Truth), section 48, Pope Benedict XVI, 2009

Suggested Topics for Reflection and/or Group Discussion

1. Identify some examples in your local or regional area where the "integrity of creation" is threatened by human actions such as pollution, threats of species extinction, significant alterations of natural features through dams or other engineering feats, etc. How does this chapter help you see the responsibility of the government, religious groups, corporations, and ordinary people regarding these and other environmental concerns?

2. Do you have grandchildren or hope to some day? Beginning with your own family, do you agree that we owe a debt of justice to future generations? To poor people in our own country and in poor nations? What could you do or what are you already doing (individually or through parish and community action) to help ensure that the poor and future generations have a just share of earth's resources?

3. Of the Christian beliefs and virtue practices discussed above, identify and mark which one(s) help you the most to deepen your understanding and appreciation of the relationships among God, humans, and the natural world.

4. What actions can you take now to increase environmental respect and responsibility—by yourself and with your family, your parish, through volunteer groups, through your local and state governments?

Action Step

This week I will....(for instance, choose one idea to learn more about, or choose to act on a justice practice suggested by the chapter narrative or the Church document summary).

Closing Prayer

Repeat the opening prayer, sing a song, or pray a prayer of your own choosing.

CHAPTER NINE

In Love With the Prince of Peace: Catholics as Peacemakers

Suggested Opening Song: "Make Me a Channel of Your Peace" (*Gather Comprehensive Hymnal* #726) or "World Peace Prayer" (*Gather Comprehensive Hymnal* #732)

Opening Prayer: Let us pray [that by growing in love...we may bring the peace of Christ to our world]

Pause for silent prayer

God our Father,
your Word, Jesus Christ, spoke peace to a sinful world
and brought [humankind] the gift of reconciliation
by the suffering and death he endured.
Teach us, the people who bear his name,
to follow the example he gave us:
may our faith, hope, and charity
turn hatred to love, conflict to peace, death to eternal life.
We ask this through Christ our Lord.

The Sacramentary, Alternative Opening Prayer, Fourth Sunday of Lent

Gospel Reading: Matthew 5:1–11 (The Beatitudes show us the way to live in order to achieve true happiness.)

Thematic Quote From Document:

In the words of our Holy Father, we need a "moral about-face." The whole world must summon the moral courage and technical means to say no to nuclear conflict; no to weapons of mass destruction; no to an arms race which robs the poor and the vulnerable; and no to

the moral danger of a nuclear age which places before humankind indefensible choices of constant terror or surrender. Peacemaking is not an optional commitment. It is a requirement of our faith. We are called to be peacemakers, not by some movement of the moment, but by our Lord Jesus. The content and context of our peacemaking is set, not by some political agenda or ideological program, but by the teachings of his Church.

THE CHALLENGE OF PEACE: GOD'S PROMISE AND OUR RESPONSE,
UNITED STATES CONFERENCE OF CATHOLIC BISHOPS, 1983,
SECTION 333, PAGE 136

Background Narrative

Try to picture Jesus riding into Jerusalem on a giant war horse on Palm Sunday. It is a jarring image, isn't it? Horses were the ancient equivalent of an army tank, while the donkey Jesus rode might compare to a minicar! Clearly Jesus was not a warrior-god, coming to vanquish the Romans and reestablish an independent Jewish kingdom, as some of his closest followers evidently hoped. In Gethsemane Jesus commanded Peter to "put your sword back into its sheath, for all who take the sword will perish by the sword" (Matthew 26:52). Then he healed the ear of the man Peter had wounded. On the morning of his resurrection, Jesus' first word to his frightened disciples was "Peace" (John 20:21). He forgave them for betraying him and running away.

Causes of war and violence: Jesus recognized the roots of war and the means of peace: As he drew near [Jerusalem] he saw the city and wept over it, saying, "If...only you knew what makes for peace—but now it is hidden from your eyes" (Luke 19:42). James 4:1–3 answers the question about where violence comes from:

Where do the wars and where do the conflicts among you come from? Is it not from your passions that make war within your members? You covet but do not possess. You kill and envy but you cannot obtain; you fight and wage war. You do not possess because

*you do not ask. You ask but do not receive, because you ask wrongly,
to spend it on your passions.*

Jesus teaches and lives peace: The gospel story of Jesus' three temptations in the desert (and his model of resistance) provides deeper answers about our disordered passions. Discord, conflict, and violence are rooted in our excessive desires and the bad deeds they lead to: lust for power over others, longing for fame and recognition, insatiable cravings for material goods and pleasures (Matthew (4:1–11). Jesus' teachings call us to love our neighbor as ourselves, to love and forgive even our enemies: "Blessed are the peacemakers, for they will be called children of God" (Matthew 5:9). His manner of life and death demonstrates a new way—a hard way—of nonviolent active resistance to evil and positive work to bring harmony and healing to all people.

The struggle to follow Christ as peacemaker in Christian history: Christians have struggled with the temptations to violence and militarism throughout our history. Many early Christian converts refused service in the Roman army. After Emperor Constantine adopted Christianity as the state religion, the Christian soldier, such as Saint Martin of Tours (d. 397), came to be honored. However, Christians (now accepting of state power) tended to forget that upon his conversion, Martin renounced military life, saying, "I am a soldier of Christ. It is not lawful for me to fight" (*The Challenge of Peace*, 1983, section 114, page 49).

The Crusades demonstrate the unfortunate consequences of "holy wars," confusing God's kingdom with the goals of one's own country or region. The Church did try over the centuries to limit violence. Saint Augustine formulated Just War principles to deter violence, and medieval Church legislation attempted to at least reduce the amount of fighting through instituting Truce of God and numerous holy days (where fighting between members of European Christendom was temporarily disallowed). But people used Just War principles to "justify" going to war, and Church leaders were not able to put an end to warfare—even between peoples who professed a common Christian faith. One of the saddest stories I ever heard was how, during World War I, soldiers from the two sides declared a truce and sang carols together on Christmas Eve, then went back to shooting each other the day after Christmas.

Death from modern war: During the twentieth century, up to 100 million people died directly from wars. Many more died indirectly from the starvation and disease that accompanied conflict. Entire cities and natural environments were also destroyed at immeasurable loss.

The rise of Catholic pacifism: In recent decades the Church has taken a significant turn from its traditional reliance on Just War principles, with a stronger call for nonviolent resolutions to conflicts. Pope John Paul II spoke out forcefully against the United States' invasion of Iraq in 2003, as well as the 1991 Persian Gulf conflict. Church teachings have also strengthened our awareness of the linkages between violence and the vast inequalities in wealth and power both within nations and between richer and poorer nations.

The contemporary Church's stronger voice for peaceful solutions flows from several twentieth-century experiences:

(1) The increasing barbarism of modern warfare, including the indiscriminate killing of innocent civilians and increasingly destructive weaponry, culminating in the invention and pro-liferation of nuclear weapons—sufficient to destroy all life on earth.

(2) The judgment that both Catholic and Lutheran Church leaders in Germany failed to adequately form the consciences of the faithful to resist the Nazi movement in Germany. One action resulting from this assessment was formation of *Pax Christi*, the international Catholic peace organization to educate and to help Catholic people work cooperatively for peace. Earlier, organized peace efforts were also developed by both Catholic and Protestant groups after World War I.

(3) The rise of Catholic pacifism (defined as nonviolent, active resistance to evil), led by the example of lay people such as Dorothy Day and the Catholic Worker movement (See Appendix C). Catholic pacifism began during World War II and continued during the Cold War, the Vietnam War, and remains active into present times. The Polish workers Solidarity movement, led by Lech Walesa, which helped bring down the Soviet Union, is the largest-scale example of contemporary Catholic pacifism. The Catholic turn toward pacifist approaches to resisting grave injustice was also deeply influenced by Gandhi's success in ending British occupation of India by peaceful resistance, and by Martin Luther King Jr.'s nonviolent Christian leadership in the African American movement for social justice in the United States. The moral power of nonviolent resistance to tyranny is increasingly apparent in numerous contemporary uprisings of oppressed groups around the globe.

Major social documents addressing war and peace: As discussed in chapter four, Pope John XXIII insisted that peace results from justice and morality in political processes, most especially from full and universal respect for universal human rights. He described the moral duties of public authorities at all levels, including international (such as the United Nations and other international treaties and covenants between nations). He addressed the needs of refugees, minorities, underdeveloped nations, and he warned about the dangers of the arms race (*Pacem in Terris*, 1963). Benedict XVI reiterates many of these themes in *Caritas in Veritate* (2009).

During Vatican II, inspired by John XXIII's leadership and the fasting and prayer of Dorothy Day and other women gathered outside, the assembled bishops strongly condemned the arms race, nuclear warfare, and genocide (Pastoral Constitution on the Church in the Modern World [*Gaudium et Spes*], 1965, sections 79, 80). They declared the arms race "a curse on the human race and the harm it inflicts on the poor is more than can be endured" (*GS* 81). Money devoted to weaponry reduces the funds available to provide for human needs. The bishops also voiced the legitimate right of conscientious objectors to refuse to participate in war-making and affirmed the teaching of John XXIII that peace can only be built on a foundation of justice and universal respect for human rights:

"Peace is more than the absence of war....A firm determination to respect the dignity of other men and other peoples along with the deliberate practice of fraternal love are absolutely necessary for the achievement of peace" (*GS* 78).

In the 1980s, extremist Cold War rhetoric and face-off "incidents" between the Soviet Union and the United States (seasoned by several Hollywood scare films) led to widespread anxiety about the real possibility of nuclear war. The U.S. government argued that our huge nuclear stockpiles were necessary as "deterrence" to Soviet aggression. In the sardonic mad-cap-comedy strain of the peace movement of the era, the policy was aptly renamed MAD (Mutually Assured Destruction).

In this tense context, the U.S. Catholic Bishops bravely issued a pastoral letter titled The Challenge of Peace (1983). It made a significant impact on public opinion by its condemnation of "first use" of nuclear weapons and blanket bombing of whole populations. Much public debate occurred about the careful statement that using nuclear weapons as "deterrence" could only be strictly, conditionally, and temporarily justified.

In 1991 (in the wake of the Persian Gulf War), Pope John Paul II made an impassioned plea to end the violence of international war:

"...War—never again!" No, never again war, which destroys the lives of innocent people, teaches how to kill, throws into upheaval even the lives of those who do the killing and leaves behind a trail of resentment and hatred, thus making it all the more difficult to find a just solution of the very problems which provoked the war (*Centesimus Annus* [On the Hundredth Anniversary], section 52).

Clergy and lay Catholics and other Christians continue to this day to witness and to work for peace in the whole world. Jim and Kathy McGinnis of St. Louis started a program to help Catholic parents learn how to raise their children as peacemakers. Kathy Kelly and Voices for Creative Nonviolence have reached out in brave solidarity with the people of Iraq and Afghanistan during two U.S. wars. Archbishop Óscar Romero in El Salvador (1980) and Bishop Juan Gerardi in Guatemala (1998) were murdered because they spoke out forcefully for the human rights and dignity of the poor in violent conditions in Central America. In 1980, four American church women also were martyred in El Salvador for their solidarity with the poor. In 1996, seven French Cistercian monks in Morocco were slaughtered by terrorists who rejected their many years of service and solidarity with their poor Muslim neighbors (Royal, 2000).

Christian witness for peace: Ordinary Christians continue to witness to the gospel and work for peace:

- educating the young in gospel values;
- witnessing and protesting at military and weapons-manufacturing sites;
- advocating against the incomprehensible level of military spending ($1.74 trillion worldwide in 2011) (Stockholm International Peace Research Institute, 2012)
- engaging in patient and sometimes risky work with the poor and disenfranchised in urban and rural areas, as well as in poor nations and underdeveloped regions of the world. For example, Catholic Relief Services maintains a presence in extremely poor and conflict-ridden places like South Sudan, Pakistan, and Haiti.

(See Appendices B and C for the names of people and organizations working for peace and human development.)

Peace based on justice is built on both personal and public efforts. Our efforts include heartfelt prayer to the Prince of Peace, practicing peaceful behavior toward family and fellow workers in our daily lives, and joining with others to challenge and change public policies that perpetuate injustice through the use of force and political power. Only when all people's basic needs are secured in a just manner will we have peace in the world and in our local communities. All Christians are called to be "blessed peacemakers."

Psalms and Scriptural Reflections

Psalm 85:1–3, 6–13 (Peace will come when we obey God's call to practice justice.)

Lamentations 3:31–36 (God has utter compassion for the afflicted and oppressed.)

Luke 22:48–51 (Jesus rebukes his followers for using violence to resist his arrest.)

Ephesians 6:10–11, 14–17 (Saint Paul uses military metaphors to encourage us to live the gospel of peace.)

The Documentary Heritage

—*The Challenge of Peace*, United States Conference of Catholic Bishops, United States Catholic Conference, 1983

This pastoral letter was written in 1983 when political tensions between the United States and the former Soviet Union were very high. The bishops held public hearings and consulted with a variety of public officials, theologians, and other experts in the process of drafting the letter. Their specific purpose was to address the dangers of nuclear war and the morality of the policy of "deterrence" or Mutually Assured Destruction (MAD) as a way to prevent a nuclear war. More broadly, the letter presents the Church's moral teachings about war, violence, and peacemaking, drawing on the life and teachings of Jesus in the New Testament as well as the experience and teachings of the Church throughout its history.

Regarding the basic moral principles, the letter states that Catholic teaching begins with a strong stand against war and a preference "for peaceful settlement of disputes" (page iii). "Offensive war of any kind is not morally justifiable" (page iv). The bishops do allow that a nation is allowed to defend itself against unjust aggression (page iv). Whether with nuclear or conventional weapons, the letter quotes Vatican II to condemn wholesale destruction of cities and civilian populations.

The U.S. and Soviet policy of "deterrence" (MAD) through the stockpiling and buildup of nuclear weapons is discussed at length. Based on careful and complex analysis, the letter reluctantly accepts "deterrence" as morally acceptable *only* as a temporary measure on the path to disarmament and peace (pages iv–v). The bishops state, unequivocally, they cannot see any situation that would justify the use of nuclear weapons: The survival of human civilization and the natural world would be at stake (section 2-A, pages 53–59).

The letter addresses the connections between peacemaking and human development by noting how the arms race robs the poor of resources that could have been used for human needs. Again quoting Vatican II, the bishops call the arms race "one of the greatest curses on the human race" (page v).

While acknowledging that military service can be carried out morally and can even contribute to peace, the bishops express their admiration for those who choose the path of conscientious objection and nonviolent means to promote peace. In addition to praising the peacemaking efforts of citizens, the letter also recommends stronger public, political commitments to peacemaking. These include: reduction and prevention of nuclear weapons; policies and education to develop nonviolent conflict resolution; establishment of global authority to address broad-based political and economic policies which improve protection of human rights; and, aid to human development (section 3, pages 86–108).

The letter concludes with a pastoral challenge to the Catholic community to engage in prayer and regular penance (such as fasting on Fridays), and to form our consciences toward closer response to the call of Jesus. The bishops call upon every diocese to establish programs to teach about war and peace in the context of Catholic commitment to promoting reverence for life (section 4-A and B, pages 115–122).

Additional Reading

—*Compendium of the Social Doctrine of the Church,* United States Conference of Catholic Bishops (Translation of Vatican document), sections 489, 494, 495; 2004

—*Centesimus Annus* (On the Hundredth Anniversary), section 52, Pope John Paul II, 1991

Suggested Topics for Reflection and/or Discussion

1. What is the most interesting or compelling new idea or new information about Christian peacemaking that you learned in this chapter? What new understanding or idea came to you. What gave you joy and encouragement? What challenged you?

2. How could the United States cooperate more with international efforts for peacemaking and peacekeeping around the world?

3. Do you agree that peace as a goal can only be achieved when human rights and human needs are met adequately? Try to think of an example of a situation where violence resulted from lack of respect for human rights and human needs. Select either an example from your own life, your local community, or from the larger world. Or, share an instance where respect for human rights and needs prevented or reduced violence.

4. How do you see the relationship between being a peacemaker in your personal life and the quest for world peace? How does trying to be a Christian peacemaker enrich your spiritual life?

Action Step

This week I will....(for instance, resolve to pray daily for peace; find out if a chapter of *Pax Christi* USA exists in your parish or local community. Consider joining or forming a new local chapter).

Closing Prayer

Repeat the opening prayer or sing the song of Saint Francis, above, "Lord, make me a channel of your peace."

CHAPTER TEN

Faith Into Action:
Living Catholic Social-Justice Values

Suggested Opening Song: "The Harvest of Justice" (*Gather Comprehensive Hymnal* #711) or "We Are the Light of the World" (*Gather Comprehensive Hymnal* #508)

Opening Prayer: Let us pray [that the kingdom of Christ may live in our hearts and come to our world]

Pause for silent prayer

Father all-powerful, God of love,
you have raised our Lord Jesus Christ from death to life,
resplendent in glory as King of creation.
Open our hearts,
free all the world to rejoice in his peace,
to glory in his justice, to live in his love.
Bring all humankind together in Jesus Christ your Son,
whose kingdom is with you and the Holy Spirit,
one God, forever and ever.

The Sacramentary, Alternative Opening Prayer, Feast of Christ the King

Gospel Reading: Mark 16:14–20 (Jesus commissions the disciples to spread the Good News to all creation.)

Thematic Quote From Document:

Listening to the cry of those who suffer violence and are oppressed by unjust systems and structures, and hearing the appeal of a world that by its perversity contradicts the plan of its Creator, we have shared our awareness of the Church's vocation to be present in the heart

of the world by proclaiming the Good News to the poor, freedom to the oppressed, and joy to the afflicted....Action on behalf of justice and participation in the transformation of the world fully appear to us as a constitutive dimension of the preaching of the Gospel, or, in other words, of the Church's mission for the redemption of the human race and its liberation from every oppressive situation.

JUSTICE IN THE WORLD, SYNOD OF BISHOPS, 1971,
BYERS, PAGES 249–250

Background Narrative

Saint James states bluntly: "Do you want proof, you ignoramus, that faith without works is useless?" (James 2:20). You, dear reader, are not ignorant: You know that living our faith in our daily lives brings life, joy, and hope for a better world that begins the reign of God announced by Jesus. Acting on our faith also brings suffering and challenges, which can only be accepted if we become people of prayer and community—relying on the grace of God and the support of our community of faith to assist us.

The influence of Catholic Social Teachings: Over the past 125 years of Catholic social-justice teaching, Church leaders and members have borne witness to these truths and accomplished much, in many different contexts. The encyclicals *Rerum Novarum* (1891) and *Quadragesimo Anno* (1931) lent major inspiration and support to workers' long struggle for justice in the factories and mines of modern industry. The U.S. Bishops' 1919 publication of *Program of Social Reconstruction* (with the assistance of Msgr. John Ryan) had a significant influence on the Roosevelt administration's policies for recovery from the Great Depression during the 1930s, especially economic security programs for the poor, elderly, and unemployed (Cort, 1988, pages 327–329; Higgins,1993).

The U.S. Bishops' 1983 pastoral letter on nuclear weapons gave much encouragement to the Catholic peace movement. Advocates for the poor in the United States and abroad were inspired by the

Church's teachings about justice for the poor and the need for a just international economic order, such as envisioned by Pope John XXIII in *Mater et Magistra* (1961) and Pope Paul VI (*Populorum Progressio*, 1967). The peoples of eastern Europe were aided in their efforts to throw off the chains of communism by the writings and speeches of Pope John Paul II. The pastoral letters and courageous witness even unto martyrdom by the Bishops of Latin America (as well as priests, religious, and lay people) contributed to improvements in democracy and living conditions in many countries (Deck, 2004; Royal, 2000).

Dorothy Day and Peter Maurin took seriously the Church's teachings on justice as guidance for their development of the lay Catholic Worker movement. *The Catholic Worker* still exists and has lay communities in most major cities of the United States. Members live simply and practice both charity and justice by their care for the poor and by their work for peace and nonviolent conflict resolution. Appendix C provides a list of social-justice saints and leaders. Learning about their lives and works can be a very inspirational way to guide your own efforts to act in Christian witness for justice in the world.

Personal and communal action: Faith-based social-justice action takes place in our personal and communal lives. It provides values and guidance for our relationships to our families and friends, to other people in the workplace, to our beliefs and actions as citizens, and in the ways we respect the earth in our use of material goods. In today's complex world, group cooperation is almost essential to make any kind of major changes. Nevertheless, we may sometimes need courage to stand up alone, trusting the Holy Spirit's hidden guidance, when a thorny ethical or justice issue confronts our conscience.

Living social justice in our personal lives: Just as "charity begins at home," so justice also begins at home. In family life the boundaries between Christian charity and justice may blur, making it difficult to perceive the difference. Regular in-depth examination of conscience —perhaps sometimes with assistance from a pastor, spiritual guide, or a friend—helps us become more honest about whether we actually give our family and friends the dignity, respect, generosity, time, and attention they have a right to expect from us.

Living social justice in the workplace: Christ calls his followers to be leaven (yeast) in the world, to help build a just social order. As employers and employees we are called to practice justice in our daily duties and in how we structure the workplace. No matter what our occupation, we have opportunities—and duties—to act justly and to offer advocacy and encouragement for just solutions to workplace challenges.

Here are just a few examples from various occupational groups of how to choose justice in practicing our occupation or profession:

- Farmers can work together through farm-based organizations for fair market arrangements for product sales and for ecologically respectful uses of soil, water, and air in their regions.
- A banker can work in good faith with government entities to set up just and helpful terms for low- and moderate-income people to obtain home and business loans, helping to change policies that enable discriminatory or greedy practices that have harmed the public.
- A young person entering the health and medical professions can choose to devote his or her life in clinics and hospitals serving poor and moderate-income populations with real and basic medical needs, rather than aspiring to practice settings that cater to the wealthy, such as cosmetic surgery or other exclusive health services.
- A lawyer or accountant can choose to prioritize service for the poor and the needs of "regular folks" versus choosing a career path oriented primarily toward personal enrichment and temptations to corruption.
- A clerk, a waitress, an office worker can make a choice to serve honestly and may sometimes be challenged to expose dishonesty or discrimination in the workplace. It is a good idea to seek good advice and support if one is in a vulnerable position.

We are called to witness by courageous behavior to just and equitable solutions to workplace challenges. Unions provide one of the ways to live out our Catholic value commitment to community: through cooperative approaches to just workplace practices. Unions also are called to work for the common good, rather than making excessive demands for wages or benefits beyond prevailing standards. Producer or consumer cooperatives are another avenue through which to promote workplace community and provide needed goods at prices fair to the workers and consumers.

Living social justice in civic action: Catholic Social Teaching supports the necessity of good government and calls all Christians to participate in politics according to their abilities to promote the common good and build a society with just laws, equitable distribution of wealth and opportunity, and services to protect and support vulnerable populations. Growing levels of extreme inequality make wealth and income distribution an urgent justice concern in American society.

Catholics are called to participate in civic life through educating ourselves about social concerns, voting, participating in public meetings, running for elective office, or helping another candidate who clearly holds a commitment to promoting policies for the common good, rather than a desire for power or public recognition. Employment in government agencies with and honesty and fairness can be an honorable way to promote justice.

We also can act for justice through nonprofit (nongovernmental) advocacy organizations. These groups work to promote just public policies through community organizing, lobbying, and advocacy efforts directed toward government or corporations that strongly affect the quality of life in our local communities (for instance, large companies or providers of public utilities such as water and energy). Some foundations currently support church-based organizing efforts in large cities to rebuild communities and promote job creation. Such advocacy activities are entirely legitimate for churches to participate in, so long as they do not support partisan (party) politics.

Living social justice through parish-based social ministry and other church organizations: The United States Conference of Catholic Bishops (USCCB) has a wealth of informational materials to foster peace and social-justice work in dioceses and parishes across the country. A particularly helpful document is titled "Communities of Salt and Light: Reflections on the Social Mission of the Parish" (usccb.org). See Appendix B for additional organizational resources.

Most dioceses, often in concert with their local Catholic Charities organization, offer resources and other hands-on assistance to parishes for living out Jesus' gospel mandate to practice justice and charity. In the vital parish we live out the mandate of Saint Paul to become the body of Christ through our care and concern for each other, through working as a parish community for justice in our local communities and nation, and indeed for the whole world.

In *Parish Social Ministry: Strategies for Success* (2001) Tom Ulrich discusses key elements of success. Several of the most basic include:

- integrating justice and charity work with the worship and full ministry of the parish.
- involving the full parish membership (not just a few ardent individuals working in a corner).
- involving persons directly affected by the problems of concern. For example, if your parish decides to work on needs of people who are homeless, families with a member experiencing mental illness, or the needs of refugees and immigrants, ask for participation by people who have actually experienced these issues. Also, seek out members of your parish who may have professional experience with responding to these needs.

Your study and prayer about the social teachings of the Church and your faithful work toward greater justice is a basic part of living out the gospel—the "glad tidings for the poor" that Jesus announced at the beginning of his public life (Luke 4:18). It is my hope that this prayer and study experience has led you to feel comfortable with the word "justice" and eager to enrich your lived faith with action for justice.

Psalms and Scriptural Reflections

Psalm 72:1–4, 7, 11–12, 14, 16–17 (Christ as king—just ruler—of the world.)

Deuteronomy 10:16–20 (God commands us to care for the weak and the poor.)

Isaiah 61:1–11 (God rejoices when we practice integrity and justice.)

Luke 6:46–49 (Acting on the teachings of Jesus makes us strong.)

Matthew 5:10 (If we suffer for justice we shall gain heaven.)

John 14:23–27 (Jesus gives us his own peace and his Spirit to guide us.)

The Documentary Heritage

—Justice in the World, Synod of Bishops, 1971

Gathered as a representative assembly of bishops from throughout the world, the Synod of Bishops voiced the remarkable commitment to justice quoted at the beginning of this chapter. Justice in the World is a brief document of four major sections.

- Section I, titled "Justice and World Society," reviews then-current world conditions: an increasingly interdependent world, thus sharing a common fate; an arms race threatening to life on earth and growing inequality in wealth. The bishops restate the Church's commitment to economic justice and the right of many disadvantaged groups to participate more equitably in economic, social, and political life.
- Section II, titled "The Gospel Message and the Mission of the Church," states that the Christian Gospel demonstrates its effectiveness through action for justice in the world. Justice enables people to recognize God as the "liberator of the oppressed" (Byers, 1985, page 255).
- Section III, titled "The Practice of Justice," calls on members of the Church to practice justice in several ways: by being just within its own activity as an employer, by educating all age

groups for justice, including exposure to actual conditions of injustice, by promoting cooperation among local churches, ecumenical partners and by supporting international agencies of international action, such as the United Nations, by promoting more respect for the natural environment.

· Section IV, titled "A Word of Hope," closes the document, reminding us, "The power of the Spirit, who raised Christ from the dead, is continuously at work in the world" (Byers, 1985, page 263).

Additional Reading

—*Mater et Magistra* (Mother and Teacher), Pope John XXIII, 1961
—*Octogesima Adveniens* (The Eightieth Anniversary of *Rerum Novarum*), Pope Paul VI, 1971

Suggested Topics for Reflection and/or Discussion

1. What have you learned from this chapter about the relationships and differences between actions of charity and actions for justice?

2. What are some things you already do to try to practice Christian charity in your life? What do you already do to try to practice justice? As a result of this study course, what more might you be willing to try to do?

3. For a group: Brainstorm ways you and your parish could practice both charitable and justice responses to a social need. For example, you could set up a prison visitation ministry through the parish and partner it with a parish advocacy plan to support prison reform. Or you could set up a parish support group for individuals and families experiencing mental illness and also advocate for better public services to help them meet their needs for housing and employment. How might you partner with existing Catholic organizations?

4. What is the best value or learning you have gained from this study course? What topics might interest you to study in more depth?

Closing Prayer

Luke 1:46–55 (Canticle of Mary, praising God's goodness, mercy, justice, and faithfulness.)

Closing Celebration

AS PEOPLE OF HOPE AND JOY, Catholics encourage celebration! If you have studied together in a group, mark the completion of this ten-part study series by planning for a simple celebration ritual. Ideas might include lighting candles and sharing an inspiring song, such as "Let Us Build the City of God" # 678 or "Bring Forth the Kingdom" #658, both in the *Gather Comprehensive Hymnal*. Dance, hug, and bless each other, share food. Celebrate in a way that feels right to your group. And remain in community with one another.

For the kingdom of God is...
of righteousness [justice], peace, and joy in the holy Spirit.
ROMANS 14:17

APPENDIX A

Global Solidarity

Seven Ways to Express Your Commitment

Action of behalf of justice and participation in the transformation of the world fully appear to us as a constitutive dimension of the preaching of the Gospel, or, in other words, of the Church's mission for the redemption of the human race and its liberation from every oppressive situation.

JUSTICE IN THE WORLD, 1971 SYNOD OF BISHOPS

1. REFLECT on Scripture and Church teachings like those discussed in this book. PRAY for inspiration and courage to express love and compassion for all people.

2. Continue to LEARN about the needs and aspirations of people in other cultures by joining with others in reading, watching documentary and feature films, attending lectures and other forms of self-education. Learn more about how rich nations are interconnected to and affect the lives of people in poor countries. Discuss with others how you might modify your own consumer spending habits to benefit people in poorer societies.

3. Reach out to meet and establish FRIENDSHIPS with individuals and families in your local community who come from other nations and cultures: immigrants, refugees, asylum seekers, exchange students, visiting professors, even tourists. Learn their stories, hopes, and desires for a good and decent life. Schools, colleges, and social agencies are good starting places to learn about newcomers in your community.

4. JOIN an ORGANIZATION that is committed to helping people in other countries. Such organizations usually publish newsletters or magazines that help you learn about conditions and needs. Examples: Religious organizations such as *Pax Christi* USA, Catholic Relief Services, Catholic Near East Welfare Association, and missionary groups such as Maryknoll; human rights organizations such as Human Rights Watch; various international women's rights organizations; and groups dedicated to helping people in one particular country (for example, "Free Tibet" or "The God's Child Project" in Guatemala).

5. Choose ONE group or issue that you feel concerned about and begin your education and involvement there. Numerous nongovernmental and nonreligious organizations are dedicated to helping specific populations (children, women, refugees, indigenous peoples), specific countries and regions (Darfur, Tibet, Colombia, the Middle East), or they are working on specific problems or needs (human rights and human trafficking, hunger, clean water, housing, AIDS, malaria, etc). Use the Internet to help with information-gathering and ideas on how to help.

6. THINK GLOBALLY, ACT LOCALLY: Encourage your parish or congregation to develop communal support projects for people in another country, such as Fair Trade Coffee (sponsored by Catholic Relief Services) or Fair Trade craft markets, The Heifer Project (sponsored by the Lutheran Church), or develop a Sister Parish relationship. Find out if your local diocese has connections with particular international support projects for churches or missionary organizations in poor nations. Join or start your own local or regional group that works on international justice issues. Study another language. Write letters to your congressional representatives in support of Fair Trade and nonmilitary foreign aid to needy countries.

7. Pray to the Holy Spirit to help you consider the possibility of doing a week, a month, or a year of VOLUNTEER work with a church or community organization in another country. Going with a church or community-based group may give you more personal support and help with integrating your experience with your Christian faith. Or consider volunteering in an inner city or at a Native American reservation to learn about poverty and cultural differences within our own country. If you can't volunteer, even an open-eyed tourist trip to places like Central America or Africa can help enhance your appreciation and understanding of other countries' needs and challenges. Try to go with a compassionate spirit, not a critical one. Resource: CatholicVolunteerNetwork.org.

Some Biblical Sources for Prayer and Reflection

- Genesis 4: We are our brothers' and sisters' keepers.
- Leviticus 25: Jubilee—forgiveness of debts, righting "wrongs."
- Isaiah 58—59: God demands justice for workers, for the poor and vulnerable.
- Matthew 25: The Last Judgment is about how we treat people in need.
- Acts of the Apostles 10: Saint Peter learns that God does not have favorite peoples.
- 1 Corinthians 12: We are all part of the one body of Christ.
- Revelation 21—22: The City of God will include people of all nations.

Resources for Catholic Social Ministries of Justice and Charity

Catholic Charities USA, 2050 Ballenger Ave., Suite 400, Alexandria, VA 22314, **catholiccharitiesusa.org**: A network of 1,700 agencies and institutions throughout the United States that seeks to "blend advocacy for those in need and public education about social justice with service to those in need." See also your local diocesan office and local Catholic Charities agency for help.

Catholic Covenant on Climate Change, **catholicclimatecovenant.org**: Provides a wide variety of information on religious response to climate change and is supported by twenty-seven national Catholic organizations, including the U.S. Conference of Catholic Bishops.

Catholic Relief Services, 228 West Lexington Street, Baltimore, MD 21201-3443, **crs.org**: The official overseas assistance organization for the Catholic Church in the United States provides both humanitarian assistance and development aid to more than 100 million people in nearly 100 countries; CRS also works for peaceful resolution of conflicts.

Catholic Volunteer Network, 6930 Carroll Avenue, Suite 820, Takoma Park, MD 20912, **catholicvolunteernetwork.org**: Helps individuals find volunteer and lay missioner placements in Catholic settings, both within the United States and abroad.

Center of Concern, 1225 Otis Street NE, Washington, DC 20017, **coc.org**: A think tank dedicated to "explore and analyze global issues and social structures from an ethical perspective based on Catholic Social Teaching." The COC sponsors Education for Justice, a website with extensive resources for prayer, study and action. Supported by the Society of Jesus.

JustFaith, **justfaith.org/programs**: Offers a wide range of study and prayer aids for an in-depth exploration of living justly.

National Catholic Rural Life Conference, 4625 Beaver Avenue, Des Moines, IA 50310, **ncrlc.com**: Addresses policy issues concerning the spiritual and justice aspects of agriculture and rural life. The NCRLC motto is "Eating is a Moral Act."

Pax Christi USA, 1225 Otis Street NE, Washington, DC 20017, **pax-christiusa.org**: United with *Pax Christi* International, *Pax Christi* USA works through both local chapters and national action to promote the Peace of Christ through prayer and action.

United States Conference of Catholic Bishops, 3211 Fourth Street NE, Washington, DC 20017, **usccb.org**: See the Office for Justice, Peace and Human Development, and the Office of Migration and Refugee Services, which offer a wealth of informational assistance, including official documents and statements issued by the U.S. Catholic Bishops on a wide range of national and international justice issues. The USCCB also has materials and consultation services to assist with starting parish social ministry activities. See especially *Communities of Salt and Light.*

Social-Justice Saints and Leaders

READING BOOKS AND ARTICLES or watching films about great leaders can be an enjoyable way to learn more about the wide variety of ways in which people have tried to live out their faith commitment to both charity and justice, in accord with the teachings of the gospel and the Church. The information here will lead you to additional resources about brave people who have worked for justice.

- Dietrich Bonhoeffer (1906–1945): A devout Lutheran minister and theologian, he helped organize and lead the "confessing" Lutheran church resistance to the Nazis. He was executed for his part in a morally controversial plan to assassinate Adolf Hitler. Bonhoeffer is a witness to the cost of true Christian discipleship. Films include *Bonhoeffer* (2003), producer/director Martin Doblmeier, available from Journey Films' website (journeyfilms.com). Books include Eberhard Bethge's *Costly Grace: An Illustrated Introduction to Dietrich Bonhoeffer* (1979), New York: Harper & Row.

- Cesar Chavez (1927–1993): A Mexican-American leader who worked to bring justice for agricultural workers, he led the long struggle to form the first union for farm workers with a strong faith foundation and commitment to nonviolent tactics. He may be considered for sainthood. Book: Roger Bruns (2005), *Cesar Chavez: A Biography*, Westport, CT: Greenwood.

- Dorothy Day (1897–1980): Founder of the Catholic Worker Movement, she modeled a life of faith linking Christian charity and action for social justice. A candidate for sainthood, she is considered by some to be the most important person in the history of American Catholicism. Film: *Entertaining Angels: The Dorothy Day Story* (1996), directed by Michael Ray Rhodes. Autobiography: *The Long*

Loneliness. Biography: Mel Piehl (1982), *Breaking Bread: The Catholic Worker and the Origin of Catholic Radicalism in America.*

- Saint Katharine Drexel (1858–1955): A wealthy Philadelphia heiress, she used all her wealth to establish schools and colleges for poor Indian and black children and fought against racism at a time when it was very unpopular to do so. Biography: Mary van Balen Holt (2002), *Meet Katharine Drexel: Heiress and God's Servant of the Oppressed*, Ann Arbor, MI: Charis Books.

- Eileen Egan (1912–2000): Cofounder of *Pax Christi*, she worked tirelessly for peaceful solutions to conflicts during her employment with Catholic Relief Services. Book: Eileen Egan (1999), *Peace Be With You: Justified Warfare or the Way of Nonviolence*, Wipf and Stock Publishers.

- Ita Ford, Maura Clarke, Jean Donovan, and Dorothy Kazel (d. 1980): These American missionaries, who worked with and for the poor of El Salvador, were raped and murdered by para-military death squads. They gave their lives, with joy, for the poor. Documentary film focused on the life of Jean Donovan: *Roses in December* (1982), directed by Ana Carrigan and Bernard Stone. Biography of Dorothy Chapon Kazel (1987): *Alleluia Woman: Sister Dorothy Kazel*, Cleveland: Chapel Publications.

- Fannie Lou Hamer (1917–1977): She went from being a poor sharecropper in the South to becoming a leading African American civil rights leader in the 1960s. Severely beaten when she first went to register to vote, she later headed up the Mississippi Freedom Democratic Party challenge to the 1964 Democratic Party convention for failure to include black representatives. Book: Bruce Watson (2010), *Freedom Summer: The Savage Season That Made Mississippi Burn and Made America a Democracy*, New York: Penguin Books.

- George Higgins (1916-2002): Known for his lifelong advocacy for justice for workers and support of labor unions, Monsignor Higgins headed the U.S. Conference of Catholic Bishops' Social

Action Department for thirty-six years. Among his many honors was receiving the Presidential Medal of Freedom in 2000. Higgins saw his work as a direct effort to put Catholic Social Teachings into action. Internet resource: Catholic-Labor Network: catholiclabor. org. Book: Msgr. George G. Higgins with William Bole (1993), *Organized Labor and The Church: Reflections of a "Labor Priest"*, New York: Paulist Press.

- Dolores Huerta (1930–): She helped Cesar Chavez found the United Farm Workers Union in the 1960s. While she struggled in her personal life (three marriages) Dolores draws on her Catholic faith for strength to continue her work for justice and nonviolent solutions to community conflicts. Book: Karenna Gore Schiff (2005), *Lighting the Way: Nine Women Who Changed Modern America*, New York: Hyperion.

- Raymond Hunthausen (1921–): The retired Catholic Archbishop of Seattle, he was both maligned and praised for speaking out against the nuclear arms buildup in the 1980s. He became an inspiration for Catholics working for world peace and an end to the arms race.

- Franz Jagerstatter (1907–1943): An Austrian farmer, beheaded by the Nazis for refusing military service, he is a profound witness to the power of faith and commitment to personal conscience. Book: Gordon Zahn (1964, 1991), *In Solitary Witness: The Life and Death of Franz Jagerstatter*, Springfield, IL: Templegate.

- Pope John Paul II (1920–2005): A major figure in the twentieth-century struggle to end communism in eastern Europe, especially in his home country of Poland, John Paul II was a tireless advocate for the dignity and equality of all humans. Book: Meg Greene Malvasi (2003), *Pope John Paul II: A Biography*, Westport, CT: Greenwood; Encyclical by John Paul: The Gospel of Life (*Evangelium Vitae*) (1995), New York: Random House.

- Kathy Kelly (1952–): She is the inspiring leader of Voices for Creative Nonviolence, a group that advocates courageously for people (especially children) affected by war, and for nonviolent solutions to Middle East and Afghanistan conflicts (vcnv.org). Book: Kathy Kelly (2005), *Other Lands Have Dreams: From Baghdad to Pekin Prison*, Petrolia, CA: AK Publishers, Counterpunch Press.

- Martin Luther King, Jr. (1929–1968): He was a spiritual and strategic leader of the 1960s civil rights revolution for African Americans and a leading voice and inspirational witness for Christian nonviolent change methods. Book (sermons and reflections by MLK): *Strength to Love* (1963, 1981), Philadelphia: Fortress Press.

- Wangari Maathai (1940–2011) led the Greenbelt movement to restore the Kenyan environment and empower poor women. Maathai was educated by Catholic sisters in Kenya and the United States in the 1960s. She became a leader for nonviolent democratic change in government. Beaten and jailed several times, she received the Nobel Peace Prize in 2004. Book: Wangari Maathai (2007), *Unbowed: A Memoir*, New York: Anchor.

- Óscar Romero (1917–1980): Catholic Archbishop of El Salvador, he was murdered in 1980 while celebrating Mass for his fearless gospel witness in support of the poor peasants against brutal government and military oppression and killings. Film: *Romero* (1989), starring Raúl Juliá, directed by John Duigan. Book: James R. Brockman (1983), *The Word Remains: A Life of Óscar Romero*, Maryknoll, NY: Orbis Books.

- Dorothy Stang (1931–2005): She was murdered in Brazil for her religiously motivated, fearless advocacy and work to protect the impoverished landless peasants of the Amazonian forests. Book: Binka Le Breton(2008), *The Greatest Gift: The Courageous Life and Martyrdom of Sister Dorothy Stang*, New York: Doubleday.

- Desmond Tutu (1931–): A South African Episcopal archbishop, he led the remarkable reconciliation movement between blacks and whites after apartheid ended, thus averting a huge bloodbath. South Africa's Christian reconciliation process has served as a model in other places, such as Rwanda. Book: John Allen (Ed.) (1994), *The Rainbow People of God: The Making of a Peaceful Revolution*, New York: Doubleday. In the book, Tutu's speeches, letters, and sermons are woven into a narrative.

References

Chapter One

Caritas in Veritate (Charity in Truth) by Benedict XVI, 2009, Washington, D.C.: United States Conference of Catholic Bishops, Publication No. 7-049.

The Challenge of Peace: God's Promise and Our Response, United States Conference of Catholic Bishops (1983), Washington, D.C.: United States Catholic Conference.

The Columbia River Watershed: Caring for Creation and the Common Good (2001). An international pastoral letter by the Catholic bishops of the region. Available from Columbia River Project, 508 Second Avenue West, Seattle, WA 98119.

Compendium of the Social Doctrine of the Church (2004), Pontifical Council for Justice and Peace, Washington, D.C. United States Conference of Catholic Bishops Publishing.

Cort, John C. (1988), *Christian Socialism: An Informal History*, Maryknoll, NY: Orbis Books.

Dignitatis Humane (Human Dignity) (Declaration on Religious Freedom, 1965), in Austin Flannery, OP (Gen. Ed. 1981 edition), *Vatican Council II: The Conciliar and Post Conciliar Documents*, Northport, NY: Costello Publishing Company, pages 799–812.

Economic Justice for All: Pastoral Letter on Catholic Social Teaching and the U.S. Economy, United States Conference of Catholic Bishops (1986), Washington, D.C.: United States Catholic Conference.

Gaudium et Spes (Pastoral Constitution on the Church in the Modern World, 1965), in Austin Flannery, OP (Gen. Ed. 1981 edition), *Vatican Council II: The Conciliar and Post Conciliar Documents*, Northport, NY: Costello Publishing Company, pages 903–1014.

Hollenbach, David (1977), "Modern Catholic Social Teachings Concerning Justice," in John C. Haughey (Ed.), *The Faith That Does Justice: Examining the Christian Sources for Social Change*, New York: Paulist Press, pages 207–231.

"Justice in the World," Synod of Bishops (1971), in David M. Byers (Ed.), *Justice in the Marketplace: Collected Statements of the Vatican and the United States Catholic Bishops on Economic Policy, 1891–1984*, Washington, D.C.: United States Catholic Conference, pages 249–263.

Mater et Magistra (Mother and Teacher), "Christianity and Social Progress" by John XXIII, 1961, in Richard W. Rousseau, SJ (2002), *Human Dignity and the Common Good: The Great Papal Social Encyclicals From Leo XIII to John Paul II*, Westport, CT: Greenwood Press, pages 133–207.

Rerum Novarum (On Capital and Labor) by Leo XIII, 1891, in Richard W. Rousseau, SJ (2002), *Human Dignity and the Common Good: The Great Papal Social Encyclicals From Leo XIII to John Paul II*, Westport, CT: Greenwood Press, pages 9–53.

Chapter Two

Augustine (1952), *The City of God* (Book 19, chapter 13), Chicago: University of Chicago.

Caritas in Veritate (Charity in Truth) by Benedict XVI, 2009, Washington, D.C.: United States Conference of Catholic Bishops, Publication No. 7-049.

Centesimus Annus (On the Hundredth Anniversary of *Rerum Novarum*) by John Paul II, 1991, in Richard W. Rousseau, SJ (2002), *Human Dignity and the Common Good: The Great Papal Social Encyclicals From Leo XIII to John Paul II*. Westport, CT: Greenwood Press, pages 433–512.

Rerum Novarum (On Capital and Labor) by Leo XIII, 1891, in Richard W. Rousseau, SJ (2002), *Human Dignity and the Common Good: The Great Papal Social Encyclicals From Leo XIII to John Paul II*, Westport, CT: Greenwood Press, pages 9–53.

Chapter Three

Caritas in Veritate (Charity in Truth) by Benedict XVI, 2009, Washington, D.C.: United States Conference of Catholic Bishops, Publication No. 7-049.

References not directly quoted

Donahue, John R., SJ (2004), "The Bible and Catholic Social Teaching," in Kenneth B. Himes, OFM (Ed.), *Modern Catholic Social Teaching: Commentaries and Interpretations*, Washington, D.C.: Georgetown University Press, pages 9–40.

Donahue, John R. (1977), "Biblical Perspectives on Justice," in John C. Haughey SJ (Ed.), *The Faith That Does Justice: Examining the Christian Sources for Social Change*, New York: Paulist Press, pages 68–112.

Chapter Four

Caritas in Veritate (Charity in Truth) by Benedict XVI, 2009, Washington, D.C.: United States Conference of Catholic Bishops, Publication No. 7-049.

Christiansen, Drew, SJ (2004), *Pacem in Terris*, in Kenneth B. Himes, OFM (Ed.), *Modern Catholic Social Teaching: Commentaries and Interpretations*, Washington, D.C.: Georgetown University Press, pages 217–243.

Compendium of the Social Doctrine of the Church, Pontifical Council for Justice and Peace (2004), Washington, D.C.: United States Conference of Catholic Bishops Publishing.

Dignitatis Humane (Declaration on Religious Freedom, 1965), in Austin Flannery, OP (Gen. Ed. 1981 edition), *Vatican Council II: The Conciliar and Post Conciliar Documents*, Northport, NY: Costello Publishing Company, pages 799–812.

Higgins, Msgr. George G. with William Bole (1993), *Organized Labor and The Church: Reflections of a "Labor Priest"*, New York: Paulist Press.

Pacem in Terris (Peace on earth) by John XXIII, 1963, in Richard W. Rousseau, SJ (2002), *Human Dignity and the Common Good: The Great Papal Social Encyclicals From Leo XIII to John Paul II*. Westport, CT: Greenwood Press, pages 209–261.

Populorum Progressio (On the Development of Peoples) by Paul VI, 1967, in Richard W. Rousseau, SJ (2002), *Human Dignity and the Common Good: The Great Papal Social Encyclicals From Leo XIII to John Paul II*, Westport, CT: Greenwood Press, pages 263–300.

Rerum Novarum (On Capital and Labor) by Leo XIII, 1891, in Richard W. Rousseau, SJ (2002), *Human Dignity and the Common Good: The Great Papal Social Encyclicals From Leo XIII to John Paul II*, Westport, CT: Greenwood Press, pages 9–53.

Stossel, Scott (2004), *Sarge: The Life and Times of Sargent Shriver*, Washington, D.C.: Smithsonian Books.

Universal Declaration of Human Rights: un.org/en/documents/udhr
usccb.org/about/migration-and-refugee-services/

Chapter Five

Augustine (1952), *The City of God* (Book 19, chapter 13), Chicago: University of Chicago.

Centesimus Annus (On the Hundredth Anniversary of *Rerum Novarum*) by John Paul II, 1991, in Richard W. Rousseau, SJ (2002), *Human Dignity and the Common Good: The Great Papal Social Encyclicals From Leo XIII to John Paul II*, Westport, CT: Greenwood Press, pages 433–512.

Economic Justice for All: Pastoral Letter on Catholic Social Teaching and the U.S. Economy, United States Conference of Catholic Bishops (1986), Washington, D.C.: United States Catholic Conference.

Chapter Six

Caritas in Veritate (Charity in Truth) by Benedict XVI, 2009, Washington, D.C.: United States Conference of Catholic Bishops, Publication No. 7-049.

Centesimus Annus (On the Hundredth Anniversary of *Rerum Novarum*) by John Paul II, 1991, in Richard W. Rousseau, SJ (2002), *Human Dignity and the Common Good: The Great Papal Social Encyclicals From Leo XIII to John Paul II*, Westport, CT: Greenwood Press, pages 433–512.

Economic Justice for All: Pastoral Letter on Catholic Social Teaching and the U.S. Economy, United States Conference of Catholic Bishops (1986), Washington, D.C.: United States Catholic Conference.

Laborem Exercens (On Human Work) by John Paul II, 1981, in Gregory Baum (1983), *The Priority of Labor: A Commentary on* Laborem Exercens, New York: Paulist Press.

Rerum Novarum (On Capital and Labor) by Leo XIII, 1891, in Richard W. Rousseau, SJ (2002), *Human Dignity and the Common Good: The Great Papal Social Encyclicals From Leo XIII to John Paul II*, Westport, CT: Greenwood Press, pages 9–53.

Chapter Seven

Deck, Allan Figueroa, SJ (2004), *Populorum Progressio*, in Kenneth B. Himes, OFM (Ed.), *Modern Catholic Social Teaching: Commentaries and Interpretations*, Washington, D.C.: Georgetown University Press, pages 292–314.

Populorum Progressio (On the Development of Peoples) by Paul VI, 1967, in Richard W. Rousseau, SJ (2002), *Human Dignity and the Common Good: The Great Papal Social Encyclicals From Leo XIII to John Paul II*, Westport, CT: Greenwood Press, pages 263–300.

Poverty Facts and Stats (7/19/2012), globalissues.org, source: World Bank Development Indicators, 2008.

Solicitudo Rei Socialis (On the Social Teaching of the Church) by John Paul II, 1987, in Richard W. Rousseau, SJ (2002), *Human Dignity and the Common Good: The Great Papal Social Encyclicals From Leo XIII to John Paul II*, Westport, CT: Greenwood Press, pages 365–431.

unhcr.org (7/10/2012), World Refugee Day, "Refugees and Forcibly Displaced Persons," source: United Nations High Commission for Refugees (UNHCR Global Trends, 2011).

un.org/millenniumgoals.

Chapter Eight

The Columbia River Watershed: Caring for Creation and the Common Good (2001). An international pastoral letter by the Catholic bishops of the region. Available from Columbia River Project, 508 Second Avenue West, Seattle, WA 98119.

Dostoevsky, Fyodor (1952), *The Brothers Karamazov*, translation by Constance Garnett, Chicago: University of Chicago Press.

Edwards, Denis (2006), *Ecology at the Heart of Faith: The Change of Heart That Leads to a New Way of Living on Earth*, Maryknoll, NY: Orbis Books.

Global Climate Change: A Plea for Dialogue, Prudence, and the Common Good, United States Conference of Catholic Bishops (2001), Washington, D.C., United States Catholic Conference.

Peace With God the Creator, Peace With All of Creation, January 1, 1990, message of Pope John Paul II for the World Day of Peace, vatican.va/holy_father/john_paul_ii/messages/peace/documents/hf_jp-ii_mes_19891208_xxiii-world-day-for-peace_en.html.

Catholic Coalition on Climate Change, ncrlc.org (6/22/2011), Weekly Update: "U.S. bishops link EPA's mercury rule with Church's pro-life agenda."

Chapter Nine

Caritas in Veritate (Charity in Truth) by Benedict XVI, 2009, Washington, D.C.: United States Conference of Catholic Bishops, Publication No. 7-049.

The Challenge of Peace: God's Promise and Our Response, United States Conference of Catholic Bishops (1983), Washington, D.C.: United States Catholic Conference.

Centesimus Annus (On the Hundredth Anniversary of *Rerum Novarum*) by John Paul II, 1991, in Richard W. Rousseau, SJ (2002), *Human Dignity and the Common Good: The Great Papal Social Encyclicals From Leo XIII to John Paul II,* Westport, CT: Greenwood Press, pages 433–512.

Gaudium et Spes (Pastoral Constitution on the Church in the Modern World, 1965), in Austin Flannery, OP (Gen. Ed. 1981 edition), *Vatican Council II: The Conciliar and Post Conciliar Documents,* Northport, NY: Costello Publishing Company, pages 903–1014.

Leitenberg, Milton (2006), *Deaths in Wars and Conflicts in the 20th Century,* Cornell University Peace Studies Program, Occasional Paper #29, third ed., http://www.cissm.umd.edu/papers/display.php?id=153 (keywords: deathwarsconflicts).

Pacem in Terris (Peace on earth) by John XXIII, 1963, in Richard W. Rousseau, SJ (2002), *Human Dignity and the Common Good: The Great Papal Social Encyclicals From Leo XIII to John Paul II,* Westport, CT: Greenwood Press, pages 209–261.

Royal, Robert (2000), *The Catholic Martyrs of the Twentieth Century: A Comprehensive World History,* New York: The Crossroad Publishing Company, chapter 13, pages 270–308.

Stockholm International Peace Research Institute (SIPRI Yearbook 2012: Armaments, Disarmament and International Security), Oxford: Oxford University Press, downloaded from sipri.org, Table 2, Military Expenditure by region, 2002–2011.

Chapter Ten

Communities of Salt and Light: Reflections on the Social Mission of the Parish, usccb.org/beliefs-and-teachings/what-we-believe/catholic-social-teaching/communities-of-salt-and-light-reflections-on-the-social-mission-of-the-parish.cfm.

Cort, John C. (1988), *Christian Socialism: An Informal History*, Maryknoll, NY: Orbis Books.

Higgins, Msgr. George G., with William Bole (1993), *Organized Labor and The Church: Reflections of a "Labor Priest"*, New York: Paulist Press.

"Justice in the World," Synod of Bishops (1971), in David M. Byers (Ed.), *Justice in the Marketplace: Collected Statements of the Vatican and the United States Catholic Bishops on Economic Policy, 1891–1984*, Washington, D.C.: United States Catholic Conference, pages 249–263.

Mater et Magistra (Mother and Teacher), "Christianity and Social Progress" by John XXIII, 1961, in Richard W. Rousseau, SJ (2002), *Human Dignity and the Common Good: The Great Papal Social Encyclicals From Leo XIII to John Paul II*, Westport, CT: Greenwood Press, pages 133–207.

Populorum Progressio (On the Development of Peoples) by Paul VI, 1967, in Richard W. Rousseau, SJ (2002), *Human Dignity and the Common Good: The Great Papal Social Encyclicals From Leo XIII to John Paul II*, Westport, CT: Greenwood Press, pages 263–300.

Quadragesimo Anno (On the Reconstruction of the Social Order) by Pius XI, 1931, in Richard W. Rousseau, SJ (2002), *Human Dignity and the Common Good: The Great Papal Social Encyclicals From Leo XIII to John Paul II*, Westport, CT: Greenwood Press, pages 55–116.

Ulrich, Tom (2001), *Parish Social Ministry: Strategies for Success*, Notre Dame, IN: Ave Maria Press.

Resources for Information and Action

Evans, Bernard F. (2006), *Lazarus at the Table: Catholics and Social Justice.* Collegeville, MN: Liturgical Press. [An easy-reading basic introduction to Catholic Social Teaching.]

Harris, Maria (1996), *Proclaim Jubilee: A Spirituality for the Twenty-First Century,* Louisville, KY: Westminster John Knox Press. [A beautifully rendered discussion of how the scriptural concept of Jubilee can be applied to debt forgiveness in our times.]

Hart, John (2006), *Sacramental Commons: Christian Ecological Ethics.* Lanham, MD: Rowman & Littlefield Publishers. [Catholic sacramental imagination and commitment to the common good form a new understanding of the sacredness of creation; includes Native American perspective.]

Henriot, Peter J.; DeBerri, Edward P.; Hug, James E.; and Schultheis, Michael J. (1985), *Catholic Social Teaching: Our Best Kept Secret.* Maryknoll, NY: Orbis Books. [A classic outline summary of key ideas in eighteen social documents.]

Himes, Kenneth R., OFM (2001), *Responses to 101 Questions on Catholic Social Teaching.* New York: Paulist Press. [Concise responses to a range of typical questions.]

Jegen, Mary Evelyn (2006), *Just Peacemakers: An Introduction to Peace and Justice,* New York: Paulist Press. [Includes many practical examples of practicing justice from a commitment to active nonviolence.]

Kammer, Fred, SJ (2004 revised edition), *Doing Faithjustice: An Introduction to Catholic Social Thought.* New York: Paulist Press. [Based on many years of experience, weds theory with many real-life examples in a readable fashion.]

Massaro, Thomas, SJ (2008), *Living Justice: Catholic Social Teaching in Action,* Lanham, MD: Rowman & Littlefield Publishers. [An accessible introduction, very suitable for classroom use in secondary or higher education settings.]

McDonald, Daniel, SJ (Ed.) (2010), *Catholic Social Teaching in Global Perspective*. Maryknoll, NY: Orbis Books. [A theological discussion among academic scholars from several regions of the world.]

Miller, Richard W. (Ed.) (2010), *God, Creation, and Climate Change: A Catholic Response to the Environmental Crisis*. Maryknoll, NY: Orbis Books. [A good basic theological study of environmental concerns by several well-known Catholic scholars.]

Simon, Arthur (2003), *How Much Is Enough? Hungering for God in an Affluent Culture*, Grand Rapids, MI: Baker Books. [A challenging and compelling call to examine our consumer habits from a Christian perspective.]